The Most Interesting People in Movies: 250 Anecdotes

David Bruce

Published by David Bruce, 2023.

THE MOST INTERESTING PEOPLE IN MOVIES: 250 ANECDOTES

First edition. June 18, 2023.

Written by David Bruce.

Table of Contents

Dedication

Dedicated to Carl Eugene Bruce and Josephine Saturday Bruce

My father, Carl Eugene Bruce, died on 24 October 2013. He used to work for Ohio Power, and at one time, his job was to shut off the electricity of people who had not paid their bills. He sometimes would find a home with an impoverished mother and some children. Instead of shutting off their electricity, he would tell the mother that she needed to pay her bill or soon her electricity would be shut off. He would write on a form that no one was home when he stopped by because if no one was home he did not have to shut off their electricity.

The best good deed that anyone ever did for my father occurred after a storm that knocked down many power lines. He and other linemen worked long hours and got wet and cold. Their feet were freezing because water got into their boots and soaked their socks. Fortunately, a kind woman gave my father and the other linemen dry socks to wear.

My mother, Josephine Saturday Bruce, died on 14 June 2003. She used to work at a store that sold clothing. One day, an impoverished mother with a baby clothed in rags walked into the store and started shoplifting in an interesting way: The mother took the rags off her baby and dressed the infant in new clothing. My mother knew that this mother could not afford to buy the clothing, but she helped the mother dress her baby and then she watched as the mother walked out of the store without paying.

My mother and my father both died at 7:40 p.m.

Cover Illustration for *The Most Interesting People in Movies: 250 Anecdotes*:

Tara Lynne Barr at the ATX Festival presentation for the TV show *Casual.*

Ms. Barr portrayed Roxy in the dark comedy film *God Bless America* (2011), earning a Young Artist Award nomination for Best Leading Young Actress in a Feature Film.

iDominick   -   https://www.flickr.com/photos/82924988@N05/27871129321/

https://creativecommons.org/licenses/by-sa/2.0/

***

This is a short, quick, and easy read.

Anecdotes are usually short humorous stories. Sometimes they are thought-provoking or informative, not amusing.

***

Educate Yourself
    Read Like A Wolf Eats
    Be Excellent to Each Other
    Books Then, Books Now, Books Forever

***

Do you know a language other than English? If you do, I give you permission to translate this book, copyright your translation, publish or self-publish it, and keep all the royalties for yourself. (Do give me credit, of course, for the original book.)

Chapter 1: From Academy Awards to Children

Academy Awards

• In 2008, Charlize Theron, 32 years old and an Oscar-winner as Best Actress in the movie *Monster*, and AnnaSophia Robb, 14 years old and the lead actress in the kids' movie *Because of Winn-Dixie*, starred together in the movie *Sleepwalking*. Normally, actors will study each other's work before acting together; however, Ms. Robb had seen very few movies starring Ms. Theron. Why? She explains, "My parents won't let me see them, especially *Monster*." In *Monster*, Ms. Theron played a street prostitute and murderer, Of course, winning an Oscar for *Monster* was very satisfying for Ms. Theron, especially because it was so hard to get the movie made and to find distribution for it. Ms. Theron says, "There wasn't one person in this industry who wanted that film made. We had our financiers calling us at 3 a.m. and asking us what the h*ll we were doing. They didn't like the way I looked [the beautiful Ms. Theron put on weight for the movie and looked ugly], and they wondered who would want to see this movie. When we finished, we couldn't pay a distributor to take it. We were hours away from signing a straight-to-video deal with Blockbuster when we found a distributor. For that reason alone, the Oscar was especially sweet."[1]

• At one time, film producer Harvey Weinstein tried to convince Barbra Streisand to star in the movie version of *Chicago*, which was to be directed by Anthony Minghella, who had just directed *The English Patient*. Always a straight talker, Ms. Streisand told Mr. Weinstein and Mr. Minghella over dinner that *The English Patient* was "overlong and overpraised." Later, of course, *The English Patient* was nominated for 12 Academy Awards and won nine, including Oscars for Best Picture and Best Director. At the Academy Awards, Ms. Streisand was seated directly behind Mr. Weinstein and Mr. Minghella. As *The English*

Patient won Oscar after Oscar, Ms. Streisand was a good sport, patting Mr. Weinstein and Mr. Minghella on the back and laughing at her critical appraisal of *The English Patient.* Mr. Minghella even told Mr. Weinstein about Ms. Streisand, "She ended up being our good luck charm."[2]

• A famous scene in the movie *Jerry Maguire*, starring Tom Cruise and Cuba Gooding, Jr., occurs when Mr. Gooding's character, a football player, makes Mr. Cruise's title character, a sports agent named Jerry Maguire, jump through a few hoops before he allows Mr. Maguire to continue to represent him. One hoop is to shout "Show me the money!" like he meant it. Jerry does that, and he gets to continue to represent Mr. Gooding's character. Mr. Cruise was nominated for an Oscar as Best Actor, and Mr. Gooding was nominated for an Oscar as Best Supporting Actor. After learning about the nominations, they got together on the telephone and shouted. Mr. Gooding says, "We screamed at each other for ten minutes. It was nothing intelligent, just 'Arrrgggghhh! Ahhh! Yeaaahhh!' I yelled. He yelled. Then he went hoarse."[3]

• Actress Angelina Jolie has the respect of people in the movie industry. In 2000, when she won a Best Supporting Actress Oscar for her role in *Girl, Interrupted*, she was making a movie titled *Original Sin* in Mexico. After flying back to the movie location following the Academy Awards, she was asleep when suddenly a mariachi band started playing outside her trailer. She went outside, where the cast and crew of *Original Sin* greeted her. Each member of the cast and crew gave her a rose—she ended up with almost 200 roses! Many of the crewmembers, including director Michael Cristofer, had worked with her before in the television movie *Gia*, and they were ecstatic that she had won an Oscar.[4]

• Harper Lee, author of *To Kill a Mockingbird*, gave Gregory Peck, who played Atticus Finch in the movie, a pocket watch that had belonged to A.C. Lee, her father, the model of Atticus. (After the book was published, friends asked A.C. to sign their copies as "Atticus," which he gladly did.) Mr. Peck was nominated for a Best Actor Oscar, and at the Academy Awards, he held that watch. He was still holding it when he won the Oscar, and he made sure to thank Ms. Lee in his acceptance speech.[5]

• Shirley Temple became a child star in movies before she learned how to read. So how did she learn her lines? Her mother read her the scripts of her movies at bedtime. In 1934, little Shirley won a miniature Oscar to recognize a major accomplishment: According to Hollywood, she had brought "more happiness to millions of children and millions of grownups than any child of her years in the history of the world."[6]

• Actress Jessica Lange has won two Oscars, and her advice to anyone who is nominated for an Oscar is to have a few words that you can say "just in case" you win. She also says that the best speech ever given by a winner was very short. Tommy Lee Jones said, "Thanks for all the work." In Hollywood, getting work is very important.[7]

• At the Oscar awards ceremony, Shelly Winters announced a winner but didn't want to hand over the Oscar, explaining, "This is very hard for an actress to let go of."[8]

Actors

• This may be a shock to some people, but at one time, two-time Oscar-winner Jody Foster thought about giving up acting. She found acting not to be rewarding anymore, and she thought about entering some other profession where she could use her analytical skills. Ms. Foster says, "I had been feeling there was something kind of not intellectually valuable about being an actor. It had started to seem like a really dumb job." Fortunately, she realized what the problem was: "It was me. It was my fault. I wasn't bringing enough to it. I hadn't realized that it was my responsibility to go deeper, to really build a character from the ground up; that to really be a good actor, you had to be able to discuss a movie, any movie that you're taking on, and to see the literature in it. *Then* it becomes fascinating. Then *you* get better as an actor. Then you learn to really love movies." With this realization, Ms. Foster rededicated herself to her career—at age 12. This paid off in a big way. Just two years later, when she was 14, she played a prostitute in *Taxi Driver*, earning an Oscar nomination.[9]

• Too often, Hollywood has stereotyped actors and actresses, sometimes because of their ethnicity. Anna May Wong played many, many Oriental stereotypes in the 1930s, something she disliked. So, of course, did other actors and actresses with Oriental features (or makeup that made them appear Oriental). Once, Ms. Wong said, "Why is it that the screen Chinese is nearly always the villain? And so crude a villain. Murderous, treacherous, a snake in the grass. We are not like that. How should we be, with a civilization that is so many times older than that of the west?" In 1960, after appearing seldom in movies for two decades, she played Lana Turner's housekeeper in *Portrait in Black*. Again, the stereotypes came out, this time from the publicity department, which explained Ms. Wong's long absence from the screen by passing along a proverb that supposedly had been taught to Ms. Wong by her mother, "Don't be photographed too much or you'll lose your soul." Ms. Wong's own explanation was different: "I was so tired of the parts I had to play."[10]

• Jeff Bridges had a good reason for wanting to star in the 1976 remake of *King Kong*: "I used to pretend I was sick whenever I saw [in] the *TV Guide* [that] *King Kong* was going to be on, so I could stay home from school and watch the original." Mr. Bridges, however, is critical of the performance of one of his co-stars in the remake. He says, "The monkey in that was just terrible. Oh, my God. Just terrible." Mr. Bridges has also seen another movie numerous times: *The Big Lebowski*, a cult favorite in which he plays The Dude. He says, "Normally when a movie of mine comes on I'll turn the channel, but when *Lebowski* comes on, I'll say, 'I'll just wait until Turturro licks the [bowling] ball, then I'll change the channel.'" But after Turturro licks the bowling ball, Mr. Bridges will say that he'll wait until another key moment in the movie occurs, and then he'll turn the channel. This keeps repeating itself until Mr. Bridges discovers that he has watched *The Big Lebowski* yet another time.[11]

• In 2007, Kenneth Branagh directed the movie *Sleuth*, with Michael Caine acting in a version reworded by Harold Pinter. Of course, Mr. Branagh has his roots in the theater, and so he used theatrical techniques in creating the movie, including two weeks of rehearsals before filming began. After the two weeks of rehearsal, everyone ran through the film one more time, with actors reciting their lines, and Mr. Branagh using a wheelchair to move Mr. Pinter to the place where the camera would be filming. Unfortunately, this made Mr. Caine nervous, and after 10 minutes of this, Mr. Caine said, "I've got to stop. I've got to stop just for one minute. I have never been this f**king nervous since I did live television. I've got f**king Harold Pinter's face about two feet from me, and above him I've got f**king Branagh giving me notes. Let me have a cup of tea."[12]

• One problem that many actors have is acting in bad weather conditions of extreme heat or extreme cold, often at unpleasant times such as night or very early in the morning. In her acting, Laura Linney deals with industrial-strength issues such as death, illness and personal failure. However, she says, "You know what's more difficult, what they don't teach you in drama school? How to act at 4:30 in the morning in the freezing cold or boiling heat. That's more challenging than any sort of emotional work. And it's like childbirth. You forget about it once a movie's finished and you're on to the next." While acting in the 2007 remake of *3:10 to Yuma*, Russell Crowe ran into the problem of an unpleasant acting environment: "We were surrounded by four-and-a-half feet of snow doing scenes where we're talking about the drought."[13]

• Script supervisor May Wale Brown was very impressed by the professionalism shown by Henry Fonda in the making of *Gideon's Trumpet*, which was a Hallmark Hall of Fame TV movie. In the movie,

Mr. Fonda used a pair of wire-rimmed glasses in his portrayal of the character he was playing. His own real glasses had heavy rims because they contained a hearing aid that he needed due to his old age. In a scene with Fay Wray, the camera focused on Ms. Wray, and Mr. Fonda was not, of course, in her close-ups. However, Mr. Fonda said his lines well, and he continued to wear the wire-rimmed glasses. When Ms. Brown told him that he could wear his own glasses (she did not want to mention the hearing aid), Mr. Fonda replied, "I want Fay to see the Gideon character when she looks at me. It'll make it easier for her."[14]

• When he was four years old, actor Steve Buscemi was hit by a bus and got his skull fractured. This doesn't mean that he was unlucky—the accident could have been a lot worse. In addition, when he became 18 years old, he received a $6,000 settlement from the city. He used the money to pay for acting school at the Lee Strasberg Institute, where he studied with John, Lee's son, who was more laid-back than his famous father. For example, Mr. Buscemi describes an acting scenario at the institute: "They had this thing where if you were in a desert and imagining sun beating down on you, you couldn't use the stage light to imagine the sun. But John said if the stage light works, that's fine. The audience don't know and don't care." Mr. Buscemi, of course, gets results, as is evidenced by his roles in such movies as *Fargo*, *Reservoir Dogs*, and *Ghost World*.[15]

• As a teenager, Scottish actor Ewan McGregor knew what he hated, and he knew what he wanted to do with his life. He hated school, and he wanted to act. His parents also knew what he hated, and they knew what he wanted to do with his life. And so one day, when Ewan was 16, his mother told him, "Look, I've spoken to your dad, and if you want to leave school you can." Lest anybody is wondering what planet his parents are from, since they allowed him to leave school, Mr. McGregor says that they are from "[t]he planet of common sense, I think. It was a wise decision. A week later I was working in Perth Repertory Theatre helping to build sets, learning my trade from the bottom up." Of course, in his case, dropping out of school worked out well, and he became a famous and successful and good actor.[16]

• Walter Slezak was an actor—he played the part of the German submarine captain in Alfred Hitchcock's *Lifeboat*. Because his father was the famous opera singer Leo Slezak, he was able to make his stage debut very early in life. At the Cologne Opera House, the director of the opera *Lohengrin* created a startling trick with perspective. At first, a boat carrying Lohengrin seemed far away, then it seemed very close to the audience. The trick worked through the use of two boats. The first boat was actually very small, and the Lohengrin seen in it was actually a child, wearing a fake beard to seem like the adult Lohengrin. The second boat was large and carried the adult tenor singing the part of Lohengrin. At one performance, the tiny but bearded Lohengrin was four-year-old Walter Slezak.[17]

• Near the end of filming the erotic thriller *Deception*, actor Ewan McGregor had to fake sexual intercourse with five different actresses, none of whom he had met before. This made him tense, but his co-star, Hugh Jackman (who played Wolverine in the *X-Men* movies) made jokes. Mr. Jackman, who also co-produced the movie, said that one of the actresses telephoned him because she was worried that she was not in the movie anymore. Fortunately, her scene had simply been rescheduled to a later date. The actress said, "I just want you to know I'll do anything, and I'm really flexible." Mr. Jackman told her that he knew that this was her first movie and it was important to her, but he joked, "I don't think she was talking about the scene!"[18]

• A couple of beefy movie stuntmen thought they could easily defeat martial arts expert Bruce Lee in a fight because he was only 5-foot-8-inches tall and weighed only 145 pounds, so he demonstrated his strength and skill to them. He placed them a few feet from a swimming pool, gave each of them an inflated bag for protection, and then told them to assume any stance they wanted. He then said that he would attempt to give one kick to each of them, without a windup or a running start, that would send the stuntmen into the swimming pool. Mr. Lee gave one kick, and the first stuntman flew into the pool, then he gave another kick, and the second stuntman flew into the pool.[19]

• In 1981, Karen Allen played the only "girl" whom Indiana Jones ever loved in *Raiders of the Lost Ark*, and in 2008 her character met the hero again in *Indiana Jones and the Kingdom of the Crystal Skull*. Of course, she was a couple of decades older, and filming took a little adjustment, although she "dove right back in, driving these big dusty, clanking old trucks on these remote locations, just like old times!" Still, Ms. Allen says, "In the beginning, I was saying, 'Oh, I don't need the knee pads. Nooo, I don't need elbow pads!' After a few days, though, you're like, 'If I put a double set on the knees, will the camera see them through my pants?' All that flinging yourself around is the hard part."[20]

• Some actors such as Chris Cooper act with reserve, using mainly their eyes to show emotion. Very often this emotion appears only on the big movie screens, not on the video monitors that many directors use. For example, during the making of *Seabiscuit*, Gary Ross, the director, would look at the video monitor, and then say to Mr. Cooper, "Y'know, I want to see a little more." Mr. Cooper would reply, "Please just go see the dailies on a big screen." Mr. Ross did, he saw the emotion he wanted, and he apologized to Mr. Cooper and then added that the next time he said, "Y'know, I want to see a little more," Mr. Cooper should "just tell me to shut the f**k up."[21]

• When comic actress Carole Lombard started filming *Twentieth Century* with John Barrymore, she was very nervous and so she was not funny. Director Howard Hawks talked to her in an attempt to get her to loosen up, and among other things he asked her what she would do if a man insulted her in a particular manner. After hearing the insult, Ms. Lombard said that she would kick the man in a very painful place. Mr. Hawks said that Mr. Barrymore was insulting her in that particular way, so she should try to kick him in that place in their next scene together.

In the scene, Ms. Lombard tried repeatedly to do exactly that—with the result that when the scene was over, Mr. Barrymore yelled, "THAT WAS FABULOUS!"[22]

• Actor Jack Nicholson is aware that two Jacks exist. Big Jack is the image, a raiser of h*ll complete with sunglasses and smokes and other stimulants. Regular Jack is a lot quieter, especially at age 70. Occasionally, people see Big Jack when Mr. Nicholson wants them to see Regular Jack. This occurs a lot with bartenders. Mr. Nicholson says, "I can't tell you how many bartenders I've had to grab by the lapel and say: 'Look, give me a very big glass with a lot of ice and a small amount of bourbon.' They see Big Jack and they want to give Big Jack that extra shot of bourbon. But you can't be Big Jack all the time."[23]

• Hollywood actress Virginia Madsen shot to fame with her role as a lonely waitress in the 2004 critically acclaimed film *Sideways*, about two men visiting the wine country of central California. She was nominated for an Oscar as Best Supporting Actress for her role. In real life, she seldom drinks wine, pointing out, "Seriously, if I buy any good stuff, it doesn't last. All my friends come over and drink it." Ms. Madsen was born on September 11, but because of the terrorist attacks on that day, she says about her birthday, "I celebrate it on a different day now."[24]

• Great art is frequently earthy. One of the most famous scenes in Ingmar Bergman's *Fanny and Alexander* shows the character Uncle Carl amusing children with his virtuoso farting; his talents include being able to blow out a candle with his wind. Was the actor who played Uncle Carl really farting? Unfortunately, no. Bertil Guve, who played the boy Alexander, explains, "They had a person sitting right next to the candle with a tube." Watch the scene carefully. When the candle is blown out, the wind does not come from Uncle Carl's backside.[25]

• Actor Jimmy Stewart once told director Peter Bogdanovich about a stranger, a fan, who told him how much he liked his delivery of a piece of dialogue that Mr. Stewart had said in a movie made 20 years previously. Mr. Stewart reflected, "And I thought, that's the wonderful thing about movies. Because if you're good, and God helps you, and you're lucky enough to have a personality that comes across, then what you're doing is, you're giving people little ... tiny ... pieces of time ... that they never forget."[26]

• Sir Laurence Olivier paid attention to the little things in his effort to make his wonderful acting even better. For example, when he was going to play Dr. Astrov in Chekhov's *Uncle Vanya*, he was extremely happy when he acquired an authentic pair of 19th-century pince-nez to wear when he played the role. He explained, "No one else might know it is real, but the fact that it is adds authority to my feeling about the role."[27]

• Actor John Hurt co-starred with Harrison Ford in the 2008 action-adventure movie *Indiana Jones and the Kingdom of the Crystal Skull*. The 66-year-old Mr. Ford had kept himself in shape, and he did his own fights and many of his character's stunts in the movie. At one point, after performing a harrowing stunt, Mr. Ford turned to Mr. Hurt and joked, "Well, you don't think they employ me to act, did you, John?"[28]

• Robert Mitchum's last movie was *Dead Man* (1995), directed by Jim Jarmusch. In it, Mr. Mitchum's character carried a big shotgun, so Mr. Jarmusch gathered together a bunch of antique shotguns, took them to Mr. Mitchum's house, and asked him to pick the shotgun he wanted to carry in the movie. Mr. Mitchum looked at the antique shotguns, then asked, "Which one is the lightest?"[29]

• Many actors, including Ryan Reynolds, who starred in the movie *Definitely, Maybe*, had a hard, penniless time breaking into show business. For a while, Mr. Reynolds and a friend lived in a cheap motel in Los Angeles, and he drove around the city in a Jeep that had been stripped by thieves and therefore lacked a few luxuries—including doors.[30]

• Jack Lemmon's first big movie was *It Should Happen to You*, starring Judy Holliday and directed by George Cukor. Jack was an enthusiastic actor, and Mr. Cukor kept telling him to act less. Eventually, Jack became upset and yelled, "If I do it any less, I won't be acting!" Mr. Cukor replied, "Exactly."[31]

Animals

• Chris Lemmon, the son of actor Jack Lemmon, wrote a memoir of his father titled *A Twist of Lemmon: A Tribute to My Father*. In the book, and in interviews about the book, he tells stories about the two of them chasing a couple of poodles through the yard of actor James Coburn. Chris and Jack look up, see Mr. Coburn glowering at them through a picture window, and they point to each other and say, "It's his fault." By the way, Mr. Coburn is actually a nice guy. Chris said in an interview that "he was just one of the biggest teddy bears you'd ever want to meet on the face of the earth."[32]

• When Yousuf Karsh went to Peter Lorre's home to photograph the famous actor, he saw a sign by the driveway: "Beware of Ferocious Dogs." The "ferocious dogs" turned out to be a couple of frisky Pekinese, a breed of very small, toy-sized dogs.[33]

Auditions

• John Cho and Kal Penn are the Korean and Indian stars of the 2004 cult movie *Harold & Kumar Go to White Castle*, but they have done much more acting than that film and its sequel. Mr. Cho played Sulu in *Star Trek* movies and appeared as a hip-hop-savvy accountant named Kenny in TV's *Ugly Betty*. Mr. Penn appeared on TV's *House* and landed a role in the dramatic movie *The Namesake* in part because of *Harold & Kumar Go to White Castle*. He explains that *Namesake* director Mira Nair let him audition because "her 14-year-old son, who was a *Harold & Kumar* fan, [...] every night before bed said, 'Mom, please audition Kal Penn for the part.'"[34]

• Laura Linney, renowned stage and movie actor, studied theater at Julliard, but like other famous actors, she went through a bad period in which she was trying to establish herself. One bad experience was auditioning for a TV commercial—during the audition this future multiple Oscar nominee had to dance around like a chicken.[35]

Automobiles

• Actress Angie Harmon started modeling as a baby—hospitals used her to demonstrate how to properly give a baby a bath. Later she appeared in advertisements for child car seats. Of course, she is beautiful, and she had gone through her geeky, awkward phase by age 12. She says, "When I was 12, I looked like I was 18. It was terrifying for my parents. I don't look forward to that with my daughters at all." By the way, as a teenager she won a contest that was sponsored by *Seventeen* magazine. Her prize was a car that sat unused for a year in her family's driveway—until she was old enough to drive it.[36]

• The makers *of Raiders of the Lost Ark* needed a 1936 German staff car for the movie, so Craig Hinton built them one by using a 1960 Jaguar chassis on which he placed a 1936 German staff car body. The movie-makers then took the car to Tunisia to film a spectacular chase scene. Immediately, the people of Tunisia treated the car with respect. Wherever Mr. Hinton drove the car, people waved at it or saluted it. Later, he learned why the Tunisians were treating the car with such respect. Tunisia had one other 1936 German staff car, and it was owned by the Tunisian President.[37]

Bathrooms

• The brother of journalist Donald Liebenson once saw actor Paul Newman at an airport and asked him for an autograph for his mother, who was a big fan. Mr. Newman replied, "Sorry, pal. Tell your mom that I don't sign autographs, but I'd be happy to buy her a beer." Years later, Mr. Liebenson saw Mr. Newman at a publicity junket and recounted that story to him. Mr. Newman replied that he could remember the exact moment that he began declining to sign autographs: "I was standing at a urinal in Sardi's, and this guy came through the door with a piece of paper. I thought this was inappropriate. It wasn't just an invasion of privacy. It was an invasion of purpose."[38]

• John Waters' very first film, *Hag in a Black Leather Jacket*, a 15-minute black-and-white movie recorded on stolen film, has an original ending. The final shot shows a piece of toilet paper on which the words "The End" have been written being flushed down a toilet.[39]

Casting

• Shawn Edwards, a movie reviewer for Fox-TV in Kansas City, loved movies from an early age. When he was in the 7th grade, he and some friends used a room at their school as a movie studio. Mr. Edwards calls the studio "the claymation joint," and he remembers, "We convinced the science teacher we were working on a science project, built these sets out of papier-mâché and started shooting our epic. It was about a group of cavemen who hunt for a dinosaur for a big celebration and please the volcano before it gets mad." When Mr. Edwards was attending Morehouse College in Atlanta, Georgia, Spike Lee filmed *School Daze* there. Mr. Edwards had broken his ankle during football practice, but he showed up at an audition for small parts and extras. He remembers that the people casting the movie looked at him as if they were thinking, "Baby, there's not a part in this movie where you can be walking around with a cast." But Mr. Edwards said, "I don't sing. I don't dance. I can't act. And I'm not that funny. I just want to be in the movie." He got lucky and appeared in a scene in which "Da Butt" was played. Mr. Edwards says, "I totally hate that song now because that's all I heard all spring. It took three freaking days to shoot" that scene.[40]

• Best-selling novelist Jackie Collins got kicked out of her school at age 15, so her parents asked her, "Hollywood or reform school?" Joan, her sister, was making movies in Hollywood, so Jackie chose Hollywood. Joan gave her a lot of freedom, meeting her at the airport and saying before disappearing, "OK, learn to drive, I can't look after you, I've got to go off on location, goodbye, here's the keys to the car, here's the list of people who can help you if you get into any trouble." Jackie says, "And I appreciated that, because [...] I was a street-smart kid, and I wanted to be by myself." For a while, Jackie appeared in movies—"always playing the Italian girl"—and she was able to take care of herself. When she went out for a part in a movie, guys would tell her, "Well, honey, let's have dinner and discuss the part." Jackie says, "And I would always say, 'Take your part for yourself,' and I would leave. So I was always that street-smart kid, you know?"[41]

• When Quentin Tarantino was casting *Kill Bill*, he held a meeting with the actors. Ricardo Montalban was supposed to be present to read the part of a Mexican pimp who was Bill's mentor, but he did not show up. Michael Parks, who was to play the role of a Southern sheriff, did show up, and he also read the part of the Mexican pimp. Mr. Tarantino liked the reading so much that he immediately hired Mr. Parks to act the part of the Mexican pimp as well as the role of the Southern sheriff. David Carradine, who played the role of Bill, was at the meeting. He remembers resolving never to miss a Quentin Tarantino meeting, and he thinks the other actors present made the same resolution.[42]

Children

• In 2008, brothers Drew and John Erick Dowdle had a hit with the horror movie *Quarantine*. They consciously modeled their careers on filmmaking brothers Joel and Ethan Cohen, with one brother studying moviemaking and the other brother studying business. After all, you have to come up with the money to make a movie before you actually make a movie. Their father, Dr. John Dowdle, an orthopedic surgeon in St. Paul, Minnesota, remembers thinking that perhaps the two brothers would not make a good team, based on their relationship while they were growing up. He says, "John was always causing Drew trouble in school. When Drew came in for freshman initiation day, they made him kneel on the floor and sing the school anthem with his head in the locker. When he finished and looked around, they were all gone." The two brothers do cast their father in their movies, but only in small parts. He mock-complains, "They haven't given me a speaking part yet. I consider that parental abuse."[43]

• In 2008, Dustin Hoffman and Angelina Jolie lent their voices to the animated movie *Kung Fu Panda*, which starred the title character voiced by Jack Black. Actually, Mr. Hoffman had met Ms. Jolie in 1991, when she was 16 years old and he was starring in the movie *Hook*. Ms. Jolie's father, Jon Voight, called Mr. Hoffman to say, "My kids are dying to meet Captain Hook. Are you in costume? Can I come over with the kids?" Mr. Hoffman agreed to meet Mr. Voight's kids, and he remembers, "So he brings over his kids. I'm introduced to his son and his daughter and she's this tall, thin, gawky-looking girl with a mouth full of braces and he introduces us." Making small talk, Mr. Hoffman asked the kids what they wanted to do. He remembers that Ms. Jolie had an answer ready: "And she gave me a laser-like intensity look and she says, 'I'm going to be an actress.' And I went home to my wife and I said, 'I don't think this kid has any idea what a tough road she's got.'"[44]

• Mary Badham, who played Scout in the movie version of *To Kill a Mockingbird*, did not want filming to end, so on the last day of shooting the movie, she deliberately flubbed several takes. However, her mother finally told her to say the lines because if shooting took much longer, the Los Angeles traffic would be very bad. During the making of the movie, the child actors frequently made Gregory Peck a target of their water pistols, so when the last take was completed, he stepped away quickly and laughed as the lighting crew poured buckets of water on the child actors. By the way, Mary was feisty. She was a 9-year-old who was playing a younger child, and when someone told her that she was little for her age, she replied, "You'd be little, too, if you drank as much coffee as I do."[45]

• Fayard Nicholas of the dance team the Nicholas Brothers loved vaudeville and hung out in the theaters, watching all the acts and learning from them. When he was 11 years old, he decided to become an entertainer, and so he created an act for himself and his brother and sister. They stayed up late rehearsing the act, and when their parents reminded them that it was a school night, Bayard told them, "We have something to show you." Their parents watched the act, then they looked at each other and said, "Hey, we have something here." Their father had them audition for the manager of the Philadelphia's Standard Theater, who quickly told him, "They're booked for next week." The Nicholas Brothers became a famous dance team in movies.[46]

• After making the movie *Get Smart*, Steve Carell, who plays Maxwell Smart, knew that his seven-year-old daughter and some of her friends wanted to see it. However, he warned her that seeing the movie might be embarrassing for her: "I had to prepare her for a scene where you see me with my trousers off. I said, 'You're going to go see this with your friends, and you're going to see my naked butt. Are you going to get embarrassed? Because you don't have to go.'" His daughter asked, "Is it funny?" Mr. Carell replied, "I think so." And she made her decision: "Well, okay then." Her decision made Mr. Carell, who values funny highly, happy.[47]

• Charles Laughton directed the movie *The Night of the Hunter*, in which an insane preacher played by Robert Mitchum chases a small boy named John, played by Billy Chapin, to get him to reveal where some money is hidden. After the film had been released, Mr. Laughton heard Mr. Mitchum ask Billy, "Do you think John's frightened of the preacher?" Billy replied that John wasn't, so Mr. Mitchum said, "Then you don't know the preacher, and you don't know John." Billy, who was somewhat cocky, said, "Oh, really? That's probably why I just won the New York Critics' Circle Prize." Mr. Laughton, hearing this, roared, "GET THAT CHILD AWAY FROM ME!"[48]

• Even when she was in kindergarten, actress Angelina Jolie liked boys. She was a member of a group known as the Kissy Girls, who would chase after the boys and kiss them—some of the boys wanted the Kissy Girls to catch them. However, at the time, Angelina's one true crush was on *Star Trek*'s Mr. Spock. Angelina also started acting when she was a toddler. Holding a video camera, her brother would tell her, "Angie, act!" Immediately, she would start acting. And her father, actor Jon Voight, would film her as she pretended to be auditioning for a role in a movie.[49]

• According to Brad Pitt, his children are "the funniest people I've ever met." For example, in 2008 his daughter Shiloh went through a phase where she wanted to be called by another name: John or Peter. Mr. Pitt calls it "a Peter Pan thing" where whenever he starts to call her by her real name she responds, "I'm John." Of course, Mr. Pitt is right when he says that this stuff is "cute to parents" and he is wrong when he says that this stuff is "probably really obnoxious to other people." It's actually pretty cute to other people.[50]

• Film director Tim Burton liked drawing and monster movies when he was a kid. When he was a 9th-grader, he entered a contest in which he created an antilittering poster. He won first prize—$10—and his poster was put on every garbage truck in Burbank, California. For a while, the young Tim's career goal was to be the actor who dressed up as Godzilla in Japanese horror movies.[51]

• Children do strange things sometimes. When he was a child, Will Hobbes, author of such young people's novels as *Beardance*, bought a ticket to a movie, and then he stood in line. When the doors opened, the line moved forward, but when young Will reached the ticket-taker, he discovered that he had been chewing on his ticket, turning it into a spitball.[52]

• The parents of Sandra Bullock, star of *Speed*, loved opera. Her mother sang, and her father taught voice. When Sandra was eight years old, she made her debut on the operatic stage: She played a gypsy child. The part was non-singing and non-speaking, but richly rewarding—members of the audience threw chocolates to her.[53]

• Mitzi Green was a child star at Paramount, and she became friends with Maxine Marx, the daughter of comedian Chico Marx. During a stay-over at Maxine's house, Mitzi put a cream on her face. Maxine asked what the cream was, and Mitzi replied, "It's a freckle remover." "Does it work?" "It hasn't yet, but I keep hoping."[54]

• Emily Watson once watched *Shrek* with her three-year-old son, who asked, "Mummy, why didn't the princess rescue herself?" As Ms. Watson points out, this "is a good question, especially as Princess Fiona is later revealed to have ninja fighting skills."[55]

• For much of his career, Steven Spielberg was known as a director of action movies for children, not as a director of serious movies. When he applied for permission to film part of *Schindler's List* at Auschwitz, he was denied permission to do so.[56]

Chapter 2: From Christmas to Education

Christmas

• One of the most famous books of Theodor Geisel, aka Dr. Seuss, is *The Grinch That Stole Christmas*, about the commercialization of Christmas. (Of course, it has also become a classic Christmas special on TV and a movie.) A couple of brothers named David and Bob Grinch requested that Mr. Geisel change the name of the lead character because they were teased about their name at school, but he declined and wrote back that actually the Grinch was a hero. True, the Grinch "starts out as a villain, but it's not how you start out that counts. It's what you are at the finish." (By the way, Mr. Geisel's license plate was "GRINCH.")[57]

• During breaks in the filming of *The Wizard of Oz*, Judy Garland used to talk to the midgets who played the Munchkins. Meinhardt Raabe remembers, "Judy was just great to us. A very pleasant young girl." For a Christmas present, Judy bought a huge box of candy and invited the little people to dig in. Margaret Pellegrini remembers, "It must have been a 25- or 30-pound box of chocolates. It was enormous. That was her Christmas present to us." Judy also brought out a stack of photographs from her dressing room and signed them for any little person who wanted one.[58]

• Hollywood scriptwriter Charlie Lederer once got angry at a producer named Sam Zimbalist, but waited four or five years before getting revenge. On New Year's Day, Mr. Lederer printed an ad in the Los Angeles newspapers and signed Mr. Zimbalist's name to it. The ad stated, "Will pay $2 for your used Christmas trees." In the ad appeared Mr. Zimbalist's address. So many Christmas trees and money-seekers descended on his home that Mr. Zimbalist was forced to go into hiding for a week.[59]

Clothing

• Many drag queens know exactly what they want, and they will go to lengths to get it. Drag queen (and Andy Warhol superstar) Jackie Curtis enjoyed wearing old ladies' clothing, and when an old lady who lived next door to her died, she went out on the ledge outside the two apartments, then broke into the old lady's apartment and burgled the old lady's clothing. And drag queen (and Andy Warhol superstar) Holly Woodlawn once wore false eyelashes, a full-length evening gown, and ostrich feathers at the welfare office to pick up her welfare check. A welfare official told her, "Sir, this is the welfare office. You're showing up in evening gown and ostrich feathers. The other welfare recipients are getting very upset about this." Holly replied, "If you buy me some jeans, I'll wear them, but I'll spend my money as I please, and I please to spend it on ostrich feathers."[60]

• In 1994, when she was acting in John Waters' *Serial Mom*, Kathleen Turner discovered that she had rheumatoid arthritis. She exercised regularly, as the doctor ordered, and she had surgery as necessary; however, for long periods of time she was unable to wear anything but slippers, although she loves shoes. In an interview with Rachel Cooke that was published in March of 2008, Ms. Turner said that she was very pleased that she had been able to wear shoes for two weeks. She had gone into a shoe store, tried a pair on, and cried, "I can wear these!" The shoe-store employee assisting her said, "Of course you can, dear." Ms. Turner admits, "I scared the h*ll out of him."[61]

• If you are really famous, it's hard to avoid the paparazzi. For a while, celebrity photographers were after all the photographs of Jennifer Aniston, Brad Pitt, and Angelina Jolie that they could get. (Actually, they are still are.) And for a while, Ms. Aniston wore the same outfit over and over, hoping that media editors would think that newly taken photographs were actually old, leftover photographs. According to celebrity photographer Gary Sun, that trick will no longer work. He says that these days the media will "use the pictures,

[and] they'll talk smack about you for wearing the same clothes over and over."[62]

• *Hollywood Reporter* publisher Billy Wilkerson discovered Lana Turner at age 16 when she was drinking a Coke at a Beverly Hills soda shop. He asked if she wanted to be in movies, and she replied, "I don't know. I have to ask my mother." Of course, she did make movies, and she did get wealthy, allowing her to indulge her desire for shoes. According to Cheryl Crane, her daughter, at one time Lana owned 698 pairs of shoes. She also had a 20-foot jewelry vault filled with precious gems in her closet.[63]

• Adrienne Janic, host of the car show *Overhaulin'* on TLC, attended the 2008 Christian Oscars: the Movieguide awards. She wore a dress with slits up the sides, and when she sat down, she used two napkins so that she would have enough material to cover up the top of the slits. Even so, one of the Christians present warned her about the evils of wearing such a dress. Ms. Janic replied, "Oh, I've got a mansion in h*ll."[64]

• In New York, Joan Collins and Bette Davis attended a Night of a 100 Stars gala. Ms. Collins was wearing a dress that she describes as "a low-cut, backless, armless, and slit-to-the-thigh silver lamé gown, created by the *Dynasty* designer Nolan Miller." Ms. Davis looked at Ms. Collins and the dress, then she told Ms. Collins, "M'dear, you almost have that dress on."[65]

• Joan Crawford often wore shoulder pads despite having big shoulders to begin with. Director Michael Curtiz disliked the look, and he once told her, "You and your damned shoulder pads," and he ripped her dress. Ms. Crawford remembered, "Then he stared in shocked amazement. The shoulders were still there. They were real."[66]

• Italian actress Silvana Mangano used to order three of each dress she had specially made for herself. At a dinner party at her home, she would disappear occasionally and return wearing a fresh dress that looked exactly like the dress she had been wearing. That way, she always looked impeccable.[67]

Comedians

• If you want people to laugh, it helps if they know that you are a comedian. For example, Groucho Marx went to a candy store and bought some candy for his children. The candy store owner did not recognize him and did not laugh when Groucho said he wanted to buy "just a few dainties to make the kiddies sick." However, later the candy store owner learned that Groucho was a famous movie comedian and so when Groucho entered the store again and said, "The kiddies want to get sick again," the candy store owner laughed hard. Groucho says, "Surely this wasn't a funny remark. Certainly it wasn't any more amusing than when I had said a similar thing before. But the fact that [the candy store owner knew that] I was a comedian made a difference."[68]

• Rick Aviles, the actor whose character killed Patrick Swayze's character in *Ghost*, once made his living as a street comedian in New York—after he passed the hat, he would find American money, francs, yen, and marks.[69]

Costumes

• A fun movie about drag queens is the Australian film *The Adventures of Priscilla, Queen of the Desert*. Directed by Stephan Elliott, the surprise international hit even won an Academy Award for Costume Design. This win is amazing: The showpiece costume of the film—the flip-flop dress—was made for only $7, thus showing the superiority of originality over money. (When the film's costume designer, Lizzy Gardiner, picked up her Oscar, she wore a dress made from credit cards.) Of course, the male stars of the film wore dresses for the movie, but for the crew photo taken after the film was completed, every member of the crew, including some very macho males, happily wore a dress.[70]

• In the summer of 2008, the blockbuster movie *Wanted* hit the screens. Based on a comic book, the movie is totally unreal, although it is more realistic than the comic book. Both the movie and the comic book feature a screen in which the anti-hero demonstrates superior shooting skill by aiming a gun at some flies and shooting only their wings off. However, the movie does not feature the comic book's costumes for the superassassins. The movie's director, Timur Bekmambetov, told comic-book artist J.G. Jones, "If there was an assassin walking down the street in a costume, everybody is going to say, 'Look, there's an assassin!'"[71]

Courts

• Of course, the movie *The Exorcist* is noted for its scenes of a possessed little girl played by Linda Blair projectile vomiting green stuff—actually, pea soup. However, it is not well known that a double named Eileen Smith was used to do the projectile vomiting. When the movie became a huge success, Ms. Smith became disturbed that Ms. Blair was getting credit for her projectile vomiting, so she sued the movie studio in an attempt to get credit for her vomiting.[72]

• Filmmaker John Waters once taught a course in prison, during which he showed some of his films. During the showing of *Female Trouble*, the convict-students watched a scene in which a lawyer argued, "If my client isn't insane, who is?" One of the convict-students whispered to Mr. Waters, "I wish my lawyer had been that good."[73]

Critics

• At the end of *The Graduate*, Dustin Hoffman's character bangs on a church window with his arms wide apart and his fingers spread open. Some critics think that they see a Christ figure in this pose, but actually when Mr. Hoffman banged on the glass with his fists, the glass seemed about to break. The pastor of the church threatened to stop the filming if Mr. Hoffman continued to bang on the glass like that, so Mr.

Hoffman spread his arms wide apart and didn't use his fists to lessen the impact of the pounding on the glass.[74]

• Often, people dislike critics, but even critics have friends. Grace Kingsley once panned a movie. The manager of a movie theater where the film was running flashed a card on the screen: "Grace Kingsley thinks this is a bad picture. What do you think?" Several of Ms. Kingsley's friends were in the theater, so they stood up and said, "We think Grace Kingsley is right," and walked out of the theater.[75]

• Violinist Mischa Elman was once present at a dinner given by Harpo Marx during which a movie producer listened to some criticisms of his recent movies, then complained of the difficulties of producing. Mr. Elman asked, "If it's so hard to make bad pictures, why don't you make good ones?"[76]

• Sylvia Miles does not suffer critics gladly. At a 1973 New York Film Festival party, she dumped a plate of spaghetti on caustic critic John Simon's head.[77]

Death

• Al Jolson was a huge entertainer in vaudeville, but his career later declined dramatically. Eventually it was resurrected when the 1946 movie *The Jolson Story*, which starred Bert Parks and won an Oscar for Best Score, came out. How forgotten was Mr. Jolson? He watched the movie in a theater, feeling very proud. At the end of the movie, which was a huge hit, people cheered, and Mr. Jolson overheard a woman say, "It's too bad Jolson couldn't be alive to see this." When Mr. Jolson was big in show biz, he was huge. He often starred in musicals on Broadway, and when he felt like it, 20 minutes into the musical, he would tell the other members of the cast, "Go home." Then he would sing and entertain solo for two hours. The audience never complained; after all, they had not come to see and hear the musical—they had come to see and hear Mr. Jolson.[78]

• Director Werner Herzog originally wanted Jason Robards to star in his movie *Fitzcarraldo*, in which a 340-ton steamship is carried over a mountain (the people involved in making the film actually did this) in the Peruvian rainforest, but Mr. Robards contracted amoebic dysentery and was unable to keep on filming the movie. Therefore, Mr. Herzog hired Klaus Kinski, whom critic Giles Harvey describes as an "incendiary, egomaniacal, tantrum-prone bull." Of course, Mr. Kinski acted in such a way as to live up to Mr. Harvey's description of him, and a Native South American chief who had been hired for the movie told Mr. Herzog that he was more than willing to kill Mr. Kinski. Mr. Herzog declined the offer although he appreciated it.[79]

• Eli Wallach played the bandit leader in the movie *The Magnificent Seven*, and in the finale, the good-guy character played by Yul Brynner shoots and kills Mr. Wallach's bad-guy character. Mr. Wallach watched the movie in a theater with Peter, his young son, who asked him, "Gee, Dad, couldn't you outdraw Yul Brynner?" Mr. Wallach replied truthfully, "One must follow the script, and if it says I get shot, I get shot."[80]

• Edmund Gwenn won an Oscar playing Santa Claus in the movie *Miracle on 34th Street*. As Mr. Gwenn lay dying, Jack Lemmon visited him and asked if dying was hard. Mr. Gwenn replied, "Oh, it's hard, very hard indeed. But not as hard as doing comedy."[81]

• Actress Joan Hackett appeared in such movies as *Will Penny* and *Support Your Local Sheriff*. Her crypt marker in Hollywood Forever Cemetery says, "JOAN HACKETT / 1934-1983 / GO AWAY — I'M ASLEEP." Jack Lemmon's grave marker in Westwood Memorial Park says only "JACK LEMMON / in" as if it were a movie credit.[82]

Directors

• Long-lived actor/director Richard Attenborough is a fountain of anecdotes. During the Second World War, his mother asked him and his brothers if it was OK with them if the family adopted two Jewish German girls. She told them, "It's entirely up to you, darling!"

Somehow, all three boys knew that she had already made up her mind to adopt the girls and that they needed to tell her that it was OK with them. All worked out well, and the girls became part of the family. Later, while he and actress Leslie Caron were making a movie together, she asked him if it was OK if she took a day off because of menstrual pains. He told her, "It's entirely up to you, darling!" Somehow, she knew that she had better not take the day off. Another of his anecdotes concerns the great character actor A.E. Matthews, who lived long and prospered, working well into his old age. Someone asked him how he did it. He replied, "'I get up, I reach for the *Times*, I look up the obituary notices, and if my name's not there, I get dressed."[83]

• Cult movie director John Waters, aka the Prince of Puke, is a true original. He writes all his scripts by hand on legal pads. He did once start to take a typing course, but the letters on the keys had all been blanked out. Mr. Waters thought that was "stupid," so he walked out. Once Mr. Waters bought some postcards of the Pope so he could use them to answer fan mail. He asked the nun selling the postcards for a receipt, but the nun told him, "The Vatican doesn't give receipts." What was Mr. Waters' reaction? He says, "I got so angry and accused her of laundering funds to anti-abortionists." Here is one more quotation from this witty interviewee. Mr. Waters says, "I don't have bad hair days. I have bad hair life. I did have long hair when I was young, but I looked like a pimp. I have instructed people to kill me if I ever wear a ponytail."[84]

• Even big-time directors like Francis Ford Coppola don't have as much power as people tend to think they do. In 1997, he wanted to cast Johnny Depp—whom he regards as "one of the three greatest actors of his generation"—as the lead in *The Rainmaker*, but the movie studio would not let him do that because at the time Mr. Depp was not the major star that he is now. Therefore, Mr. Coppola had to tell him, "Listen, they absolutely forbid me to cast you in this." Mr. Depp replied, "But we thought you were a god!" Mr. Coppola says, "A lot of people think that being a name director, you do absolutely what you want to do and only what you want to do. Maybe Steven Spielberg's earned that right with his extraordinary career. But he would be the only one who has that type of power."[85]

• Controversial film director John Waters finds inspiration for his films in real life. In a Baltimore bar, he once asked a man what he did for a living. The man replied, "Can I be frank? I trade deer meat for crack." Mr. Waters reflects, "I can't think that up. I could think of three movies about him. I mean, does he wait at a deer crossing sign and gun it when he need[s] a fix? It takes a while to get deer meat so you have to plan ahead, which isn't what most junkies do. Little things like that, anything can inspire me. I base everything on regular people who think they're completely normal and their behavior seems entirely insane to me."[86]

• Film director Robert Altman had an old Iranian-born friend named Reza Badiyi, who became a television director. They once went on a cross-country trip and ended up in Las Vegas without any money. Mr. Altman convinced a Las Vegas hotel that Mr. Badiyi was actually a famous Middle Eastern prince who lived large and whose name was currently in many gossip columns. The hotel gave them free room and board. However, the real Middle Eastern prince showed up at the hotel. Fortunately, he thought that what the two friends had done was funny, and he and Mr. Badiyi partied together in Las Vegas.[87]

• Werner Herzog, the director of *Fitzcarraldo*, *The Enigma of Caspar Hauser*, and *Aguirre, the Wrath of God*, has advice on how to become a successful filmmaker: "Work as a bouncer in a sex club, work as a taxi driver, work as a butcher—earn the money and make your own film." Perhaps his most important advice is to make a film instead of making excuses for why you can't make a film. He says, "Today, with these little digital cameras, there is no excuse any more." Mr. Herzog himself stole his first camera and used it to make 11 films. He says about the camera, "It fulfilled its real destiny."[88]

• Director Charles Laughton chose silent film star Lillian Gish to be one of the stars in his movie *The Night of the Hunter* (1955). When she asked why he had chosen her, he replied, "When I first went to the movies, people sat in their seats straight and leaned forward. Now they slump down, with their heads back, or eat candy and popcorn. I want them to sit up straight again." Mr. Laughton's film, with its moody atmosphere and gripping performances, is exactly the kind of movie to make people in the audience sit up straight in their seats again.[89]

• Penny Marshall directed *Big*, a movie for which Tom Hanks was nominated for a Best Actor Oscar. Later, she directed *A League of Their Own*. Mr. Hanks wanted the role of the drunken coach of one of the women's baseball teams, but he had a nice-guy image and Ms. Marshall was reluctant to give the role to him. However, she agreed to give him the role on one condition—he had to apologize to the other actors for the last five films he had made, films that were not as good (in most people's eyes) as *Big*.[90]

• Alfred Hitchcock claimed that he was misquoted when an article stated that he had said, "Actors are cattle." Mr. Hitchcock insisted that what he had really said was, "Actors should be treated like cattle." According to movie lore, Carole Lombard, the actress he was currently working with, led several cows onto the set for him to direct, and then she went home.[91]

• Ridley Scott has directed many different kinds of films including *Alien*, *American Gangster*, *Blade Runner*, *Gladiator*, *Hannibal*, *Matchstick Men*, and *Thelma and Louise*. As you would expect, he watches many, many films. At 11 p.m. he starts watching a movie, and he says that "if I'm still watching at 1, that means it's a good film."[92]

Education

• Not every family is happy. While growing up, actor Corbin Bernsen did not have a really good relationship with his father, and at one point, during the process of getting a divorce, his mother was drinking way too much. In addition, Corbin was going through a process of teenage rebellion and blaming his parents for it. Corbin says, "I was a typical kid, getting high and acting crazy. And I said, 'Well, Mom is this' and 'I do this because of that' and 'What do you expect?'" His father then taught him an important lesson. Corbin remembers, "My dad said, 'You have a choice in life. You can be happy or you can be sad. But don't blame anybody else other than yourself. If your life is going to be screwed up, don't blame me or your mom.'" He decided to become an actor after seeing his mother on the stage in a production of *The Miracle Worker*, following which he thought, "Wow, that's my mother up there, the crazy woman who makes my dinner. Look at what she's doing!'" She also taught him an important lesson: "She said, 'I don't mind you following what I'm doing. You've seen the ups and downs. The only thing I demand of you is that you love and respect your craft. It doesn't matter if you're doing a commercial or a movie, just love it. Love all of it.'"[93]

• Censors can come up with some funny things to object to. For example, in the early 20th century, a Midwestern women's organization objected to the nudity of the Walt Disney cartoon character Clarabelle Cow. Fortunately, this objection was easy to disarm. Mr. Disney simply drew the character a skirt to wear. By the way, being able to draw a convincing cartoon character takes both talent and lots of study. For example, Disney artists study movies of a cow. At first, the cow is a calf, then it grows up, and then it is milked. By studying the movie, Disney artists discover such things as this fact: "Look! No matter how fat a cow gets, her hips still stay bony." Another artist discovered this fact: "When she eats, she moves her jaw from side to side instead of up and down the way we do."[94]

• Kenny Ortega was able to choreograph the movie *Dirty Dancing* because he had relevant experience from high school. Whenever a new hot record came out, he and his friends would meet and play the record over and over—sometimes 50 times—before the next Friday night's dance. Those dances were known for their bottled-up sexual tension.

Mr. Ortega says, "It was not uncommon for our high-school dances to be shut down because of all the gyrating and rubbing up against each other. The vice principal would routinely come out on the stage and announce, 'If there is any more dirty dancing in here, the dance will be cancelled.'"[95]

• One of the best things that ever happened to director Roman Polanski was something he failed at. He had early success in acting, and when he applied to an acting school the directors turned down his application, saying that his professional experience had "distorted" him. This rejection motivated Mr. Polanski to succeed as a way to get revenge. He says of the rejection, "That was one of the greatest failures in my life, comparable with anything that ever happened afterwards in my professional life, and it gave me tremendous confidence and push, doubled my energies to get back at them."[96]

• More dance performances ought to be preserved on film and video. Why? Here's one reason. Ballerina Ghislaine Thesmar was inspired to pursue ballet seriously after her dance teacher showed her a film of Russian ballerina Galina Ulanova dancing the title role in *Giselle*. According to Ms. Thesmar, "I was simply overwhelmed. I suddenly saw what dancing could be. It was watching Ulanova that completely changed my life. From that moment on, I realized that dancing could hold real meaning in one's life. I could see the dimension that a life in dance could offer. Suddenly, I knew what I wanted."[97]

• Arnold Schwarzenegger has exhibited much drive in his life. One person who taught him to accomplish much was Franz Steeger, a boy in Arnold's village who held the record for chinning himself on a tree limb: 21 chin-ups. The 14-year-old Arnold tried chinning himself, and he did 18 chin-ups, but Franz told him, "You do the rest with your mind." Franz gave him a pep talk, and Arnold tried again. He did 18 chin-ups, then he did a difficult 19th chin-up, and then Franz reminded him, "You do the rest with your mind." Arnold kept going, and he broke the record with 22 chin-ups.[98]

• When she was a little girl, actress Samantha Morton attended drama club with other little kids. For one lesson, she was supposed to improvise a scene with another little girl. The two girls stood in front of the group, and the drama teacher whispered to little Samantha the theme of the improvisation: "The other girl's stolen your hamster." Samantha responded by improvising in her own way. She says, "I beat the crap out of this girl, and they didn't ask me back."[99]

• Movies can have a major effect on private life. For example, Cary Grant starred in many romantic movies. According to movie critic Pauline Kael, boys of her day learned from Cary Grant's movies. His characters were always suave when they went on dates with women, and she remembers, "Every boy became a better date."[100]

Chapter 3: From Fame to Language

Fame

• For 50 years, actor Paul Newman and his actress wife, Joanne Woodward, lived in Westport, Connecticut. He blended in, and Westport residents respected his privacy. He ate at the Westport Pizzeria and took his grandsons trick-or-treating in town. Once, he climbed to the top of a stockade fence and yelled, "Hi, I'm Paul Newman, your neighbor. Seen my dog?" He did get involved in politics to a limited extent, campaigning for some candidates. Once, he even pretended to be a robo-call—a taped recording telephoned to many thousands of people—and telephoned several people just to see what would happen. What happened? People hung up—quickly.[101]

• Some superstars enjoy fame. When silent-movie greats Douglas Fairbanks and Mary Pickford got married, they went to Europe for their honeymoon, where they were at first astonished by the mobs of people who recognized them. Therefore, they slipped away to Germany, where they were not nearly so well known. After a while, though, they decided to go back to where they had been mobbed. Ms. Pickford said to her new husband, "Let's go someplace where we are known. I've had enough obscurity for a lifetime."[102]

Family

• Working on a Farrelly brothers movie such as *There's Something About Mary* can be a fun experience. For one thing, the Farrelly brothers hire a lot of family and friends—and not just their own—as extras. For example, *There's Something About Mary* starred Cameron Diaz, and her father makes an appearance in a scene in which co-star Ben Stiller is in jail—Cameron's father's character has silver-streaked long black hair. Cameron's mother was also offered a small part in the movie, but she turned it down. By the way, when Cameron was auditioning for her first movie—*The Mask*, starring Jim Carrey—she discovered that the movie-makers were looking for someone more voluptuous than she. Because she was thin—in high school her nickname was Skeletor—she worried that she did not have the female frontal development the movie-makers were looking for, so she invested $36 in a padded bra—and got the part.[103]

• Elliott Gould, of course, is a famous actor who has made many movies, including those in the *Oceans* franchise. His daughter, Molly, was shopping with Elliott's soon-to-be five-year-old granddaughter, whose name is Daisy, at a Wal-Mart. Molly was looking at videos, and when she saw a DVD of *Oceans Thirteen*, whose cover showed Mr. Gould, she said, "Oh, look, there's Grandpa." Daisy replied, "*Our* grandpa?"[104]

Fans

• In 1981, three boys aged between 10 and 11 in Mississippi decided to do a shot-for-shot video remake of Stephen Spielberg's *Raiders of the Lost Ark*. The three boys were Eric Zala (director of *Raiders of the Lost Ark: The Adaptation*), Chris Strompolos (the video remake's producer and star), and Jayson Lamb (the video remake's special-effects wizard). Chris knew that Eric was a fan of the movie, and, as the now grown-up Eric explains, he invited him to help create the remake: "I imagined that the sets were all built, the costumes were all picked out, and I'd just walk onto the set and help out. Little did I know that at the time, all that Chris had done was buy the script at Waldenbooks and cast himself as Indiana Jones." The kids thought that doing the remake would take all summer, but it ended up taking seven summers. Eric was a first-year student in college by the time it was done. Of course, creating a 100-minute remake of *Raiders of the Lost Ark* using your allowances takes a lot of low-budget ingenuity. Exotic locations were made out of cardboard, and the Nazis were played by tweens wearing their Boy Scouts uniforms. They didn't have a trained monkey to use for comic relief, so they used a dog named Snickers. What about the boulder in the famous opening sequence? That took a lot of work. They made the first "boulder" out of duct tape and bamboo poles; unfortunately, they made it so big that they couldn't get it out of the bedroom they had made it in. They made the second "boulder" out of chicken wire; unfortunately, it was so light that a hurricane blew it away. Third time's a charm. Their fiberglass "boulder" still exists; it sits in Eric's mother's backyard. They finished editing in 1989. (Mr. Spielberg has seen and liked the video remake, and he has met Mr. Zala, Mr. Strompolos, and Mr. Lamb.)[105]

• At age five, Leonardo diCaprio was thrown off the set of *Romper Room*. Why? He was too rowdy. Since then, he has come up in the acting world. Claire Danes, who starred with him in Baz Luhrmann's *Romeo + Juliet*, said about her female fans, "They just like me because I got to kiss Leo in *Romeo + Juliet*." Of course, *Titanic* was a huge money-maker with Leonardo as the romantic lead, and of course, with a monster hit like *Titanic*, Leonardo can do pretty much what he wants to do. *Entertainment Weekly* wrote about him after *Titanic* came out, "After *Titanic*, DiCaprio could probably sell tickets to a documentary about belly button lint." Mr. DiCaprio is capable of great sensitivity toward his fans. At the premiere of *The Man in the Iron Mask*, to which he took his mother, a young fan got close enough to him to touch his hand. The fan says, "He just turned to me and said, 'Hi. How are you doing?' and he held my hand for a second. Then he actually apologized because he couldn't stay. He said he had to get his mother inside. I couldn't believe how polite and calm he was with all those people screaming his name."[106]

• A woman named Suki, whose birth name was Deanne Newbury, is a true fan of cult movie director John Waters. Visitors to her house have to recite a line from one of his movies before she lets them in. Sometimes, she won't let in a visitor even if the visitor recites a line. For example, Robrt L. Pela wanted to interview her while he was researching his book *Filthy: The Weird World of John Waters*. He recited this line from the movie *Pink Flamingos*: "Nobody sends you a t*rd and expects to live!" However, Suki shouted, "DO YOU HAVE ANY

IDEA HOW MANY PEOPLE HAVE BROUGHT ME THAT QUOTE? YOU'LL HAVE TO COME BACK ANOTHER TIME. SORRY." She had several John Waters posters displayed in her office at work, something a supervisor criticized her for, so she took down the posters and put up this sign in its place: "If you can find some other miserable b*tch to work here for sh*t wages with a bunch of squares, hire her." The next day her boss called her and asked her to come back to work. Suki even keeps a shrine to John Waters in her bathroom.[107]

• Harry Knowles, who writes for <aintitcool.com>, is a geeks' geek. He was able to be in China for part of the filming of Quentin Tarantino's *Kill Bill*, and of course he wrote about it for his Web site. At one point in the film, actor David Carradine, who played Bill, had to throw a knife. His wife, Annie, moved away from the set because, she said, "I know how he throws." Harry, however, stayed close by the camera so he could be close to the action, saying, "If I get killed by a knife thrown by David Carradine, I'll be a happy man." Another time, David's character was supposed to slit a man's throat, spraying fake blood everywhere. Again, Harry stayed close to the action. Asked whether he wanted to move further away, he said, "Are you kidding? You think I'm going to miss getting blood sprayed on me by David Carradine? That's what I came to China for!"[108]

• A man by the name of Joseph Cornell was infatuated by an actress named Luise Rainier, who had won Oscars for her work in *The Great Ziegfeld* and *The Good Earth* and who was living in Switzerland. Each year, Mr. Cornell made and sent her a carefully crafted box. She never acknowledged the gifts, but simply put them in a closet. When she sold her house, she threw away 20 of Mr. Cornell's boxes. Back in New York, she was walking down a street when she came across an art gallery advertising James Cornell boxes. Because the art gallery was closed, the following day she phoned an art museum to find out how much a James Cornell box was worth. She learned that Mr. Cornell was a famous

American artist and sculptor, and she learned that she had thrown away approximately $20 million of his art.[109]

• Christopher Reeve, star of four Superman movies, played a bigamist whom fans loved to hate on the soap opera *Love of Life*. Some fans of the soap confused the character he was playing with the real-life Mr. Reeve. Once, he was eating lunch in a restaurant in Manhattan when an angry fan hit him on the head with her purse. Benjamin, his brother, looked like him, and an angry fan once hit him on the back with her umbrella.[110]

• Movie star Clark Gable once arrived late for an appointment to have his portrait taken by renowned photographer Yousuf Karsh. Why? He had been stuck in an elevator for nearly an hour at a department store on Wiltshire Boulevard. For Mr. Clark, being stuck on an elevator was a minor annoyance, but his fans who were stuck on the elevator with him were delighted.[111]

• Marilyn Monroe had many fans who loved—and obeyed—her. While making *Some Like It Hot* on a public beach, Ms. Monroe was watched by hundreds of fans, who could occasionally be noisy. However, whenever it was time to film a scene, director Billy Wilder would ask Ms. Monroe to say "Shh" to her fans, and they immediately quieted.[112]

Fathers

• In 2008, *People* magazine named Hugh Jackman the sexiest man alive. Also in 2008, his children, Oscar and Ava, were three years old. Neither of them liked to take baths because that meant that the day was coming to an end and they would have to go to bed soon. Therefore, he invented "Make Time." He says, "We throw pillows. I swing them around. We play hide and seek for a half hour. By the time we're finished, they're totally exhausted and crawl into the bath. If you came over to our house at about 6:30 in the evening, you'd hear me say, 'Are you ready for Make Time?'"[113]

• Hollywood actor Jeff Bridges' father is Hollywood actor Lloyd Bridges, which means that Jeff believes, "I'm a product of nepotism. I was carried onscreen when I was 6 months old." Because Lloyd really enjoyed acting—actually, he took joy in life itself—he encouraged his children, including Jeff's older brother, Beau, to go into acting. Jeff says that "like most kids, I rebelled against my parents. But he'd say, 'Well, you get to get out of school.'" Sure enough, after making approximately 10 movies, Jeff decided that he wanted to act as a career.[114]

• When Alec Baldwin and his brother Daniel were kids, they wanted to take tennis lessons from local athletic champion Jimmy Luchsinger, who was teaching tennis at a nearby park, but they lacked tennis rackets. Their father brought home a pair of tennis rackets for them, saying, "If you miss one lesson, I'll be very upset with you." Alec remembers seeing his father lying on the couch—his shoes had holes as big as half-dollars in them. He says, "The man who would not resole his shoes had given us the rackets. That was my dad."[115]

• Tim Roth is mainly known as a character actor and as the undercover cop ("Mr. Orange") who got shot in the gut in Quentin Tarantino's *Reservoir Dogs*, but he got the chance to be a star in the 2008 summer blockbuster *The Incredible Hulk*, in which he played the villainous Emil Blonsky. Why did he take the job (besides the paycheck)? He has sons: 12 and 13 years old. They attended the Los Angeles premiere and gave it thumbs up. Mr. Roth says, "They really loved it. I'm the cool dad now. Brownie points."[116]

• When Steven Spielberg was six years old, his father, Arnold, who was a scientist, woke him up late at night to see a meteor shower. This experience stayed with young Steven, and as an adult, he placed lights streaking across the sky in a scene of his movie *Close Encounters of the Third Kind*.[117]

Food

• How did Sandra Bullock know that she had really, really made it as a movie actor? While making the movie *Demolition Man* with

Sylvester Stallone, she engaged in conversation with producer Joel Silver about the best kind of marshmallow fluff—she thinks that the best kind comes in a plastic jar rather than in a glass jar. She happened to mention that she would like a fluff sandwich, which is made with peanut butter and marshmallow fluff, and three days later, a crate of marshmallow fluff appeared as a gift for her. She says, "They couldn't get it out in California, so they had somebody look for it on the East Coast and flew it out."[118]

• When Groucho Marx, star of such movies as *Horsefeathers* with his famous brothers, was a young man in vaudeville, he once worked at an Atlantic City theater whose manager also ran a boarding house on the waterfront where entertainers stayed. This manager was a man who knew how to save a dollar. Every meal featured fish because outside Groucho's window, the theater manager kept a huge fishing net into which Groucho's breakfast, lunch, and dinner swam. Perhaps unnecessarily, Groucho says that after his engagement at the Atlantic City theater was over, for an entire week he ate nothing but roast beef.[119]

• Theodor Geisel, aka Dr. Seuss, disliked making the movie *The 5,000 Fingers of Dr. T*, and the critics hated it, but it did provide one happy memory for him. The movie featured 150 boy pianists, and one day the movie studio made the mistake of giving the boys' weekly salary to the boys instead of to the boys' parents or agents. The boys happily gorged themselves on way too many hot dogs and way too much other junk food, and then filming resumed. One boy vomited, and this caused a chain reaction, as one boy after another upchucked the results of a junk-food orgy.[120]

• One thing Paul Newman cared about strongly was salad dressing, and salad dressing was the first product that appeared under the brand name "Newman's Own." Early in his marriage to Joanne Woodward, they went on a date to Chasen's, a very fancy Los Angeles restaurant. She remembers, "It was one of our first stylish meals out, and he took an already oiled salad to the men's room, washed it clean, dried it with towels, and returned to the table to do things right, with oil cut by a dash of water."[121]

• While Michael Kidd was choreographing the movie *Guys and Dolls*, Samuel Goldwyn wanted to take him out for a meal, so he asked him if he liked Jewish food. Mr. Kidd did, so Mr. Goldwyn took him to Lindy's, raving on the way about Lindy's delicious Jewish food: gefilte fish, kishke, kneidlach, kugel, lockshen, and so on. Arriving at Lindy's, Mr. Goldwyn asked the waiter what the special was. The waiter replied, "Irish stew," and Mr. Goldwyn said, "That's what we'll have."[122]

• When Bob Hope was making short comic films for Vitaphone studio head Sam Sax, the movie crew wasted little time—they sometimes made a short in three days. According to Mr. Hope, "If we fell behind schedule, we got a three-minute lunch period. If we really fell behind, Sam put a lunch scene in the picture, and we ate while the cameras rolled."[123]

• Christopher Reeve, who played the title role in four Superman movies, played an important role in the movie *The Bostonians*, partly because the movie's co-producer, Ismail Merchant, bribed him—with a weekly home-cooked Indian meal. After the movie's filming was done, Mr. Merchant gave Mr. Reeve a T-shirt that said, "I did it for curry."[124]

Friends

• Steven Spielberg and George Lucas worked together to create *Raiders of the Lost Ark*. Mr. Spielberg did the directing, and Mr. Lucas, the producer, occasionally visited on location. Sometimes they would have minor disagreements. Mr. Lucas would give in and say, "Well, it's your movie. If the audience doesn't like it, they're going to blame you." And Mr. Spielberg would joke, "OK, but I'm going to tell them that *you* made me do it."[125]

• When friends Walter Matthau and Jack Lemmon made the movie *Buddy, Buddy*, Mr. Matthau took a bad spill on the set. Worried, Mr.

Lemmon folded his jacket and tenderly put it under Mr. Matthau's head and then asked, "Are you comfortable?" Mr. Matthau replied, "I make a living."[126]

Gays and Lesbians

• The mother of comedian Liz Feldman knew that Liz was a lesbian even before Liz figured it out. At age 16, Liz went away from home to a summer drama program at which a girl seduced her. Liz knew then that she liked girls, but at the time she thought she also liked boys. The following summer she went to another drama program, and her mother walked into Liz's room and saw two girls sleeping together in bed. Ironically, the girls weren't gay; they were just tired. One month later, Liz stayed the night at one of the girls' houses, and when she returned home her mother told her, "There's a letter on your bed … it's from me." Her mother also told her, "Don't open it here—open it in the car!" In the car, which Liz was not allowed to drive, she opened the letter, in which were two poems. The first poem was written from the perspective of a daughter who comes out to her mother and says that she's gay. Not ready yet to talk, Liz simply told her mother, "You're very perceptive." The second poem was written from the perspective of a mother talking to her gay daughter, saying, "It's OK, we'll figure it out, I still love you." Both poems rhymed. Liz didn't want her mother to tell her father, who believed that being gay was a mental disease, but her mother told her father anyway. Her father took her to get a psychiatric evaluation, and the therapist asked, "What's the problem?" Liz replied, "That's just it. I don't think it's a problem. Everybody else thinks it's a problem, but I just wish we would stop using the word 'problem.'" Liz is justly proud today of how she handled this situation at age 17. After the psychiatric evaluation, Liz says, "The therapist said I was the most mentally stable teenager she'd ever had in her office and that I didn't need therapy, but that she recommended that my parents stay on" to get some help in adjusting to their daughter's gayness. Her father was proud of Liz's psychiatric evaluation. He told her, "Most mentally stable kid, look at you!" He also tossed her the keys to the family car, and that was the first time she was allowed to drive it. As a 30-year-old adult, Liz made this coming-out story into a short movie. To protect his privacy, her father does not appear in the film, which is titled "My First Time Driving." Liz says, "I made the film with my sister, which was also a dream come true. I always wanted to work with my sister; we're very close and get along really beautifully."[127]

• Pratibha Parmar, the director of *Nina's Heavenly Delights* and other movies, finds her content in subjects such as lesbians, women, and South Asians. She has a happy relationship with her partner, and her movie *Nina's Heavenly Delights* tells a positive lesbian love story. She says, "In my own life I have a very happy, full relationship with my partner. I've had that for many years, and I know many other lesbians who do, so why do we always have to be portrayed as psychos or dysfunctional women? Why [are we not portrayed] just like anyone else? We fall in love and yeah, we go through our struggles, but also we have a potential to live happily ever after." By showing positive portrayals of lesbians, *Nina's Heavenly Delights* reflects reality. For example, in the summer of 2006, Ms. Parmar and her partner attended a civil partnership ceremony for two lesbians they know. She says, "The two women were both Indian, and they'd had their outfits made and embroidered in India. Both their families were there, their uncles and their aunts and their mums and dads and their nephews, kids running around. It was like a typical Indian wedding except that there were two brides. Now that is progress. That is change. So my film [*Nina's Heavenly Delights*] isn't just complete fantasy; things like that do happen."[128]

• George Takei's fellow actors on *Star Trek* accept his homosexuality. (Mr. Takei played Sulu on the original TV series of *Star Trek*.) When the *Star Trek* movies began to be made, Mr. Takei would bring his partner, Brad Altman, to the Friday-night wrap parties after a week's work was done. The first time he introduced Mr. Altman as a "friend," but he kept bringing Mr. Altman to the parties. Mr. Takei says about his fellow workers in TV and movies, "They're sophisticated people, so they put two and two together and said, 'Hmmm, I get it.'" He discovered that Walter Koenig, the actor who played Pavel Chekov, knew that he was gay when Mr. Koenig motioned for him to turn around one day. Mr. Takei did turn around, and he saw a "stunningly good-looking young extra wearing the tight *Star Trek* uniform." Immediately, Mr. Takei thought, "Okay, Walter knows and Walter understands." Mr. Koenig and his wife also invited Mr. Takei over to visit them, saying, "Why don't you bring Brad over?" Therefore, Mr. Takei says that his outing "happened in a very normal, natural, friendly way."[129]

• One of *Tucson Weekly* columnist Tom Danehy's friends was an almost flamboyantly gay man also named Tom, who worked a couple of days a week at Blockblocker in addition to holding down another job. Gay Tom was a movie buff. Mr. Danehy says that often customers would come in looking for something like *Saw XXVII* but gay Tom would convince them to rent a true suspense classic such as *Dial 'M' for Murder* instead. In fact, gay Tom would follow customers around in the video store, and he would often say about a customer's choice, "Don't take that!" Then gay Tom would guide the customers to the "classics" section and convince them to rent something that truly exemplified excellence.[130]

• Movies are rated G, PG, R, and X; so are movie trailers. Gay comedy writer Bruce Vilanch noticed that the movie trailer for *Chasing Amy* was rated R because of a brief kiss between two women—the trailer had no violence, drug use, or bad language. However, movie trailers rated G showed such things as dinosaurs trying to eat people, men with guns shooting other men with guns, and people screaming as their cars head straight toward a cliff.[131]

• Gays and lesbians can be *Star Wars* fanatics, too. In England, a lesbian couple wanted their wedding cake to display the Death Star from the movie *Star Wars*. The bakery at first declined to create a cake like that, until one lesbian exclaimed, "Look, it's my big gay wedding and we want a Death Star!" By the way, model makers created the spaceships for George Lucas' *Star Wars* by using parts from model kits for such vehicles as Kenworth Tractors, Panzer Kampfwagens, a Ford Galaxy 500 XL, and Kandy-Vans.[132]

Good Deeds

• Some actor/directors are very giving of their time. Actor Thomas Jane has worked in the films *The Punisher* and *Deep Blue Sea*, and he starred in the HBO dramatic comedy series *Hung*. When he decided to direct and star in the straight-to-DVD thriller *Dark Country*, he telephoned Mel Gibson, one of the most successful actors and actor/directors ever. Mr. Jane explained that his thriller would be straight to DVD, but Mr. Gibson still spoke to him for over an hour on the phone and gave him the benefit of his experience and advice. Mr. Gibson also said that the first time he both directed and starred in a movie, he telephoned actor/director Clint Eastwood, who passed on some advice from the man whom *he* had telephoned the first time he both directed and starred in a movie: Don Siegel. Mr. Siegel told him, "Don't sell yourself short. Take time for yourself, as much time as you take for all the other actors and all the other aspects of production; spend as much time on yourself as you do on those people."[133]

• Celebrities often move in the same circles. Just before graduating from high school, actress Jennifer Love Hewitt was being driven around in a car that would next be used to drive around actor Johnny Depp, a fact that Ms. Hewitt learned from talking to the driver. She asked the driver to tell Mr. Depp "Hi" for her. Apparently, the driver also told him that Ms. Hewitt was graduating. Quickly, Ms. Hewitt received a message on her answering machine: "My brother wants to send you flowers. Please call with your address." She did call and asked, "Who is your brother?" The answer? "Johnny Depp." And yes, Mr. Depp did send flowers to her when she graduated.[134]

• When Audrey Hepburn was a chorus girl, celebrated photographer Antony Beauchamp wanted to photograph her. Ms. Hepburn told him that she could not afford his fee, but Mr. Beauchamp photographed her without charge. Years later, she requested that he be the photographer for stills of a movie she was shooting in Italy. Another important gift came later, from Gary Cooper, whom Ms. Hepburn worked with and greatly respected. After Mr. Cooper died, his widow sent Ms. Hepburn his 24-carat cigarette lighter, a gift she cherished.[135]

• Famed photographer Yousuf Karsh once played tennis with a partner who promised him a kiss from "one of the most famous actresses in Hollywood" if he were to win the match. Motivated greatly by this promise, Mr. Karsh did win the match, and as promised Joan Crawford kissed him and served him cocktails. In addition, she always sent him a handwritten personal note on such occasions as his birthday and important holidays.[136]

• When Fay Kanin started writing for the movies, she told her boss, Sam Marx, the story editor at MGM, "Mr. Marx, I know you own *Gone with the Wind*. I've read it, and I would be a wonderful writer for it." He smiled at her brashness and said, "I think they have in mind a more expensive writer for it." Ms. Kanin always appreciated that he used the word "expensive" instead of the word "talented."[137]

• Movie star Bette Midler uses topical and local humor in her nightclub act. As she tours, she calls up gay hot lines and gay switchboards to get the names of local homophobes so she can make fun of them in her act in that city.[138]

Halloween

• While creating *E.T. the Extra-Terrestrial*, director Steven Spielberg worked with young children, including a six-year-old Drew Barrymore, and so he wanted to make the filming fun. On Halloween, he went to work dressed up in costume—as a woman. Drew remembers, "He looked great!" He was also filmed in costume, and he said to the camera, "This is Halloween, folks. I don't dress this way *all* the time."[139]

Husbands and Wives

• Bob Balaban is both an actor and a director. He acted in such movies *as Midnight Cowboy, Close Encounters of the Third Kind, Prince of the City, Waiting for Guffman,* and *Gosford Park,* and he directed the HBO movie *Bernard and Doris,* starring Ralph Fiennes and Susan Sarandan. In addition, he has been married since 1977 to Lynn Grossman, a former classmate who has had two children with him. His advice about having a long and successful marriage is to find "something deeply interesting about each other." Note that he does NOT say that the secret to having a long and successful marriage is to "fall in love with each other at first sight." That definitely did not happen in their case. Mr. Balaban says when they were taking classes together, "She kind of thought I was a homeless person. I used to smoke a lot and dressed in army camouflage outfits and was always running out of money. She thought I was a sad character."[140]

• While Andre Previn was married to Mia Farrow, he belonged to the Garrick Club. One day, the club secretary invited him to bring Mia to dinner there, but added, "By the way, you must forgive me for this, but she can't use the main staircase. The women have to go round the back." This shocked Mr. Previn, and when he told his wife about the invitation— and about women not being allowed to use the main staircase—she replied, "You have 10 minutes in which to quit the club." Fortunately, he had the perfect reply: "I've already done it." Years later, Mr. Previn said, "Unbelievable. Mia was the wrong person to try that on."[141]

• When Walter Slezak decided to become an actor, he went to Berlin with a letter of introduction to a famous and much-married actor named Paul Wegener. Because Mr. Slezak knew that actors sleep late, he arrived at Mr. Wegener's house at 12:30 p.m. At 3 p.m. Mr. Wegener got out of bed with a hangover. After learning that Mr. Slezak wanted his advice, Mr. Wegener replied, "I have good advice for you, real good advice—DON'T EVER MARRY." Mr. Slezak quickly left.[142]

• Actress Greer Garson married Buddy Fogelson, a Texas oil millionaire. When he was serving as an officer in the United States, he visited a movie set where Ms. Greer was working, and he started talking to her, although he did not realize that the attractive redhead was Greer Garson. Soon, he announced, "You're the one I'm going to marry. I don't care about meeting the real Greer Garson."[143]

• Eli Wallach's first movie was *Baby Doll*, which co-starred another actor with a notable nose: Karl Malden. Mr. Wallach and his wife, Anne Jackson, saw the movie in a theater. The first time that Mr. Wallach and Mr. Malden appeared on the screen together, Ms. Jackson whispered to her husband, "Never have two noses filled the screen so completely."[144]

• Alfred Hitchcock's *Psycho*, in which the character played by Janet Leigh is murdered in a shower, caused many people to be afraid of taking a shower. One man wrote Mr. Hitchcock to complain that his wife was now afraid to take a shower or a bath. Mr. Hitchcock wrote back, "Sir, have you ever considered sending your wife to be dry-cleaned?"[145]

• Actress/dancer Ann Miller had a fabulous career, but was unlucky in love. A millionaire husband of hers kept mistresses, which Ms. Miller could not accept. She told her husband, "Either they go, or I go!" He responded, "Pack your bags."[146]

Language

• Sometimes Arnold Schwarzenegger says exactly the wrong thing; sometimes he says exactly the right thing. When he met Dino De Laurentiis, who produced the Schwarzenegger movie *Conan the Barbarian*, Mr. Schwarzenegger was shocked that Mr. De Laurentiis was such a small man, so he asked, "Why does such a little man like you need such a huge desk?" His agent later told him, "That was the worst thing I ever heard anybody say when he's trying to get a job." One time when Mr. Schwarzenegger said exactly the right thing was when he was hit with an egg while he was campaigning for governor of California. He said, "That guy owes me bacon."[147]

• Movie actor Ewan McGregor's wife is a French woman named Eve (pronounced Ev) Mavrakis. One result of this is that their daughter's first words were in French, not English. Therefore, Mr. McGregor decided to learn more French; otherwise, when his daughter grew up and argued with him, he might not understand some of the words she used. By the way, when Mr. McGregor got married in France, one of the few French words he knew was "oui," which he spoke when prompted. Also by the way, Mr. McGregor, who played a younger Obi-Wan Kanobi in the prequel *Star Wars* movies, slept on *Star Wars* sheets when he was a kid.[148]

• Nikolaj Coster-Waldau, who is Danish, starred as an immortal New York police officer in Fox's TV series *New Amsterdam*. He is multilingual and has acted using many languages, but of course he does not have equal facility in all of the languages he speaks. For example, his French can be lacking. Mr. Coster-Waldau remembers one particular movie: "The script was in French, and I learned all my lines. I was working with this actress who was great, but she wanted to improvise. All I could do is look at her with great depth in my eyes."[149]

• The family of comedian Mike Mycrs, star of the *Wayne's World* and *Austin Powers* movies, came from Liverpool, England, although he was born and raised in Canada. Because the Beatles, who came from Liverpool, sounded so much like his parents, when Mike was very young, he thought that he was related to the Beatles. By the way, after Mike married Robin Ruzan, they had three dogs, but Mike declined to reveal the dogs' names to the media—out of fear that the dogs would be dognapped.[150]

Chapter 4: From Letters to Parties

Letters

• For a while, writers Ben Hecht and Charles MacArthur ran a movie studio in which they produced their own scripts. They had a policy of not responding to letters, instead hiring someone to burn their mail each day, unread. However, they did read a letter from a movie theater owner in Iron Mountain, Michigan, which was printed in the *Exhibitors' Herald*, a movie trade magazine. The letter complained that the Hecht-MacArthur movie *The Scoundrel* was bad for business and annoying to the Iron Mountain movie-goers. Hecht and MacArthur spent all day composing an insulting letter, saying among other things that the citizens of Iron Mountain were so backward that they lived in trees. After mailing the letter, Hecht and MacArthur read the reply in the next issue of the *Exhibitors' Herald*. The movie theater owner had written, "Messers Hecht and MacArthur, I have received your letter, framed it and hung it in the lobby of my theatre, where it is attracting a great deal more attention than did your motion picture."[151]

• Meredith Willson, the author of *The Music Man*, says that he was in movie mogul Sam Goldwyn's office when a secretary came in and said, "Mr. Goldwyn, the filing cabinets are full of so much correspondence that I have no room for anything. Will you allow me to sort out the old letters and burn them?" Mr. Goldwyn replied, "Of course, I wish you would—but be sure to keep copies."[152]

• Early in her career, Audrey Hepburn attended a Screen Actors Guild at which Marlon Brando was present. She was in awe of him and said hello, but after that they did not speak to each other. Forty years later, Mr. Brando wrote a letter in which he explained why he had not spoken to her. He had been unable to speak because he held her in such awe.[153]

• John Waters is the filmmaker who made the infamous *Pink Flamingoes*, as well as several other films that celebrate trash. Once, he received a letter from a teenager who wrote him, "I'm in high school, and I make films like you do. How come I get sent to the school psychiatrist and you get sent to Europe?"[154]

Media

• An advantage of being a journalist is that you may occasionally get to interview actors you adore. For example, when *Guardian* reporter Libby Brooks was 13, she saw *Dirty Dancing* on video and fell in love with Johnny Castle, who was played by Patrick Swayze. Lots of young girls who saw the movie, including Ms. Brooks, wanted to lose their virginity to Johnny Castle. Years later, she got to interview Mr. Swayze, who repeated for her his famous line from the movie: "Nobody puts Baby in a corner." Ms. Brooks' interview with Mr. Swayze was never printed, and she admits today, "In retrospect, I think that my editor was less interested in Swayze than in bringing an end to my relentless badgering to let me interview him." The movie's rating prevented many girls from seeing the movie in theaters—they had to wait to see it on video. This meant that some girls were able to be cool by seeing the movie in theaters. Ms. Brooks remembers when a French teacher asked Lindsay Cameron in class, *"Lequel est le dernier film tu as vu?"* (What is the last film you saw?). Ms. Cameron confirmed her status as the coolest girl in class by replying, "Le *Dirty Dancing*."[155]

• Charles Foster Kane in Orson Welles' *Citizen Kane* was based on William Randolph Hearst, a fact that embittered Mr. Hearst. After *Citizen Kane* had been made, and after Mr. Hearst had set his newspaper battalions against the movie, Mr. Hearst and Mr. Welles met on an elevator, and Mr. Welles invited Mr. Hearst to attend the San Francisco premiere of *Citizen Kane*. Mr. Hearst ignored him and got off the elevator. Mr. Welles shouted after him, "Charles Foster Kane would have accepted."[156]

• Even John Wayne was a victim of the scandal sheets during his illustrious career. One scandal sheet printed some horrible allegations about Mr. Wayne's wife and her ex-husband, so the ex-husband shot and wounded the reporter. When the media asked Mr. Wayne what he thought about it, he replied that he wished the ex-husband had been a better shot.[157]

Mishaps

• In the movie *Titanic* is a scene in which the character played by Leonardo DiCaprio sketches the character played by Kate Winslet while she is nude. Before the scene was filmed, Mr. DiCaprio walked into the place where Mr. Winslet was being made up—while she was nude. Mr. DiCaprio said, "Whooa!" But Ms. Winslet said, "We're going to spend the whole day like this. We might as well get used to it." By the way, Mr. DiCaprio got his first name because while his mother was pregnant with him, she and her husband were walking through the Uffuzi Museum in Florence. While looking at a painting by Leonardo da Vinci, she felt her baby kick, so she decided to name him after the famous painter. Leonardo diCaprio's middle name is Wilhelm; he was named after his maternal grandfather, Wilhelm Idenbirken.[158]

• During the filming of *The Wizard of Oz*, a few mishaps occurred. For example, the teacher who taught child actors thought that the adult midgets who performed as the Munchkins were children and tried to round them up and take them to school. And one wardrobe lady asked an adult little person to undress, saying, "I have a little one just like you at home." When the little person undressed, she realized from the physical evidence that she was in the presence of an adult male.[159]

• Playwright Charles MacArthur was rewriting a speech in his play *The Front Page* when producer Jed Harris walked in, and looked over his shoulder at the writing. Mr. Harris said, "That's no good," then yanked the paper out of the typewriter. Mr. MacArthur let out a roar of rage and started for Mr. Harris, who ran for his life as *Front Page* co-writer Ben Hecht restrained Mr. MacArthur. Later, Mr. MacArthur and Mr. Hecht added this scene to their play.[160]

• In 1974, at a movie theater in Rio de Janeiro, an usherette interrupted a showing of *The Exorcist* by chasing a rat across the stage. Members of the audience wanted her—and the rat—off the stage, so they started yelling, "Take them off!" Misinterpreting their cries, the usherette did a strip tease and she was dancing naked when the police arrested her. Later, she explained, "I thought the audience was calling for me. I was as surprised as anyone."[161]

• Hollywood cameraman James Wong Howe had the greatest amount of fun in his career during the days of silent movies. He remembers driving around with a crew looking for a house to shoot in front of. If no one was home, they began to shoot the film. If the homeowner returned before they had finished, everyone would hop over the fence and take off running as if they were in a Keystone Kops comedy.[162]

• This anecdote is interesting rather than funny. Making movies can be hazardous. Joseph Fiennes, star of the movie *Shakespeare in Love*, also made the movie *The Great Raid*. For that 2002 film, which was made in Australia, he attempted to surf 15-foot waves, but a wipe-out ripped off one of his lips, an injury that necessitated a graft from one of his earlobs. These days, he is seldom photographed without facial hair.[163]

• Movie producer Marcel DeSano once tried to commit suicide by turning on the gas and suffocating. He planned almost everything in detail. He taped the windows shut, he sprayed perfume around the room, he put on a favorite record, he turned the gas on, and he lay down and went to sleep. However, he woke up again, very much alive—he had forgotten to pay his gas bill.[164]

• In 2006, six weeks after Melissa Rivers, the daughter of Joan Rivers, had given birth, she attended a televised event (with a celebrity red carpet) at which someone looked at her and asked her when her baby was due. Fortunately, George Clooney came up to her. Melissa says, "He put his arm around me and said I looked amazing. That made me feel so much better."[165]

• To celebrate Kate Moss' 22nd birthday, Johnny Depp threw a big party for her at the Portobello Hotel in Notting Hill. He even ordered that a bathtub at the hotel be filled with champagne. Unfortunately, while he was busy elsewhere, a chambermaid entered the room and pulled the plug in the bathtub.[166]

• Filming *The Texas Chain Saw Massacre* was dangerous. In one scene, Gunnar Hansen (playing Leatherface) was running with a whirling chain saw when he slipped. The whirling chain saw flew in the air and landed a few inches from Mr. Hansen's body.[167]

• In the movie *Words and Music*, Vera Ellen did knee slides with Gene Kelly. Because she didn't know how to do the knee slides correctly, the following day her knees looked like basketballs.[168]

Money

• When making the movie *Definitely, Maybe*, 11-year-old actress Abigail Breslin spent some time bonding with actor Ryan Reynolds, who played the father of Abigail's character. At one point, they went to a toy store together, and Ryan offered to buy her any toy she picked out. Big mistake. Abigail chose a huge stuffed furry lion, and when Ryan went to the checkout counter, he found out its price was $300! Later, after the purchase had been made, Abigail herself found out how much the stuffed animal had cost, and shocked, before she could stop herself, she exclaimed about the purchase—and purchaser, "Three hundred dollars on a stuffed toy? What an idiot!" Of course, she was grateful for the gift, but still shocked, she points out, "I've never even seen $300!"[169]

• Frank Sinatra spent money freely. A valet once brought him his car, and Frank asked him what had been the biggest tip he had ever received. The valet replied that it had been $100. Frank gave him a

$200 tip, and then he asked the valet who had given him the $100 tip. The valet replied, "You did, sir. Last week." Sammy Davis, Jr., imitated Frank's free-spending ways, with the result that he met with an accountant, who advised him to cut down on his expenses or face financial ruin. The next day, Sammy sent the accountant a gift: a gold Cartier cigarette case inscribed, "Thanks for the advice."[170]

• Groucho Marx was occasionally afraid of losing his stardom and his money. In his autobiography, *Groucho and Me*, he explains how this fear started. While working on a movie titled *A Day at the Races*, the director, Sam Wood, said to him, "Groucho, you see those women over there? Well, ten years ago, twelve of the fourteen were stars and earned fifteen hundred dollars a week and more. Today they're extras, getting ten and a half dollars. Pity, isn't it?" As soon as the day's shooting was done, Groucho rushed to the phone, called his insurance agent, and bought an annuity to provide for his old age.[171]

• When Joel and Ethan Coen made the movie *No Country for Old Men*, about the aftermath of a drug deal that goes wrong in the Texas desert, they ran into a very high expense. The film required many extras—who were covered in "blood"—to lie on the desert ground for hours. The Coens discovered that they needed to buy specially made "blood" for $800 a gallon instead of using the usual inexpensive "blood" made with Karo syrup and red food coloring. They couldn't use the sugary "blood" because it would have attracted many, many creepy-crawlies.[172]

• During the Great Depression, movies were a wonderful source of inexpensive entertainment; still, some movie theaters had promotions to encourage people without much money to watch movies. Often, a piece of pink dinnerware (now known as "Depression glass") was given away with every movie ticket purchased. In the 1930s, one movie theater, owned by the father of June Lassack, gave away envelopes filled with money. Most envelopes contained only pennies, but a few envelopes contained $1 or even $5.[173]

• Controversial film director John Waters has many talents, including the ability to give an entertaining pitch to people who may invest money that he can use to make his movies. Once he wrote a screenplay about a skinhead invasion of a community, and he pitched it to Dawn Steel of Disney, who listened to him, then joked, "Well, *sure*, when I heard 'skinheads,' I thought Disney!" Mr. Waters says, "She knew that they weren't going to do it, but I give an entertaining pitch, so she took the meetings anyway."[174]

• Many movie actors make big money but worry about what will happen when they cease to be stars. James Cagney, the owner of a substantial fortune, once confessed to Spencer Tracy that he was one such worrier: "How can I know whether I'll have any money 20 years from now? How do I know whether even the Motion Picture Actors Home will take me in?" Mr. Tracy replied that there was one way to be sure that the Motion Picture Actors Home would take him in: "Buy it now."[175]

• Two characteristics of screenwriter Wilson Mizner were that he was outspoken and he enjoyed having money. Early in his Hollywood career, he moved quickly from one studio to another, but at 20th Century Fox he received his first paycheck, opened it, then pretended to be a great hurry. A friend asked where he was going, and Mr. Mizner replied, "To the doctor. I want him to paralyze the muscles that move my head sideways. From now on I want to nod only up and down."[176]

• Tom Hanks, of course, has won back-to-back Oscars for Best Actor for his roles in *Philadelphia* and *Forrest Gump*. This puts him in the ranks of actors who can command millions of dollars for starring in a movie. However, like most other actors, he underwent a period of poverty before making it big. Early in his career as an actor, his sister returned several empty soda-pop containers for the deposit so that she could send him an admittedly small amount of money.[177]

• In 1967, struggling Canadian actor Donald Sutherland wanted to go to the United States to seek work, but he lacked money, so he made an appeal to established actor Christopher Plummer. Quickly, Mr. Sutherland learned that Mr. Plummer had given him a loan, placing $1,500 in his bank account. The money allowed Mr. Sutherland to get a good start on his acting career in the United States, but it took him five years to pay back the money.[178]

• As an eight-year-old girl, Tatum O'Neal made *Paper Moon*; for a while afterward, her father, Ryan O'Neal, would not let her make any more movies. However, one day a teenaged Tatum told him that she wanted to use her earnings from *Paper Moon* to buy a horse ranch. He explained, "You made only $16,000. That won't buy it." Soon after, Tatum made $350,000 (and got a percentage) by acting in *The Bad News Bears*.[179]

• Tobey Maguire plays Spider-Man and Peter Parker in the movies. His parents were unmarried, and they split up when he was two years old. At first, he wanted to be a cook like his father, but his mother, a secretary, said that she would give him $100 if he took a drama class in high school. He did take the class, he enjoyed it, and for acting in *Spider-Man*, he made $4 million—for acting in *Spider-Man 2*, he made $17 million.[180]

• While filming the B horror movie *Evil Dead* in rural Tennessee, actor Bruce Campbell withdrew some money from a local bank, then realized that it smelled funny. He told the bank teller, "This money smells like dirt." She wasn't surprised, saying, "Makes sense. Folks around here still bury it in their backyard."[181]

• French comic filmmaker Jacques Tati had a Dutch grandfather named van Hoof, who ran a Parisian picture-framing shop. One of his customers was Vincent van Gogh, who frequently offered to pay his bill with one of his paintings. Unfortunately, Mr. van Hoof insisted on being paid with money.[182]

• Spike Lee made his first feature film, *She's Gotta Have It*, for $175,000 at a time when the production of some TV commercials cost more than that. Money was so tight that he told his actors not to throw away their soft drink bottles so he could return them for the deposit.[183]

• When he was 12 years old, Denzel Washington worked in a barber shop, cleaning up, running errands for patrons, and whisking away stray hairs after patrons had haircuts. He appreciated the tips he made, and he admits, "Everybody looked like a dollar bill to me."[184]

Mothers

• Ryan Gosling has played many troubled characters in his acting career, including a Jewish neo-Nazi in the movie *The Believer*, a movie that his mother, Donna, was able to watch for only 10 minutes before bursting into tears and running into the bathroom. Mr. Gosling was able to convince her to come out of the bathroom—but it took him an hour. A few years later, she was much more comfortable with his acting career, so comfortable that she did not freak out when he started sleeping every night with a sex doll by him to prepare himself for his leading role in the movie *Lars and the Real Girl*, about a troubled man who thinks that a sex doll is a real girl. Mr. Gosling says, "My poor mother, she doesn't ask questions any more. She just says, 'Oh yeah, sex-doll movie. It's great!' She's a really supportive mom."[185]

• Stuart Hample turned Woody Allen, whose standup comedy he had enjoyed, into a comic strip in the 1970s. Mr. Allen approved the comic character, and they worked together on the jokes, which included some of Mr. Allen's standup material. Mr. Hample wondered why Mr. Allen had approved the comic strip, but of course there were advantages. For example, Mr. Allen cast the actress Mary Beth Hurt as the sister of the character played by Diane Keaton in his movie *Interiors*. Ms. Hurt telephoned her mother and said that she was going to be in a movie "by somebody you probably haven't heard of, a director named Woody Allen." Her mother replied, "I know about him. He's in the funny pages."[186]

• In 2000, Jon Chattman got his first real movie-star interview. He was assigned to write an article about filmmakers Robert Benton and

Joseph L. Mankiewicz, and he telephoned several movie stars, leaving messages to call him back so he could interview them. The one movie star who called him back was Paul Newman. However, when Mr. Newman called, it was Mr. Chattman's mother who answered the phone. As Mr. Chattmann reconstructed the telephone call later, it went something like this: "Hello, is Jon Chattman there?" "Who's calling?" "Paul Newman." "The Paul Newman?" "Yes." "Wow! This is his mother. I love you."[187]

• The young Bette Davis went through a period of false glamour—briefly—after becoming a star. With a fancy car, a liveried chauffer, and a white poodle, and wearing fancy black velvet slacks and a fancy black velvet jacket, Ms. Davis ran into her mother, who stared at her and told her that she could not believe what her eyes were telling her. Fortunately for fans everywhere, Ms. Davis jettisoned the false glamour before that day ended and went back to being herself.[188]

• In the 1970s, actor Donald Sutherland, star of *M*A*S*H*, was both a cinematic icon and a sex symbol; however, some people may consider him an unlikely sex symbol. When he was in his teens, he asked his mother if he was handsome. She replied, "Donald, to be perfectly truthful, no. But your face has a lot of character."[189]

• After Cameron Diaz graduated from high school, she signed with a modeling agency and began to travel around the world to model in exotic locales. Her mother gave her a gift at the beginning of her career: a long silver hairpin. Why? If necessary, it could be used as a weapon. Cameron says, "Moms are like that."[190]

• Actress Noreen Nash, one of the stars of *Giant*, found it easy to decide to give up shooting on location. After shooting a movie, she returned home and discovered that her two-year-old son barely knew who she was.[191]

Music

• David Raskin was a music composer for the movies. One day, a couple of friends teased him, saying that his work was unimportant.

After all, the great director Alfred Hitchcock had decided not to have any music in his new movie, because it took place on a lifeboat, and there wouldn't be any music out there—where would it come from? Mr. Raskin replied, "You go ask Mr. Hitchcock where his cameras come from out in the middle of the ocean and I'll tell him where the music comes from."[192]

• A Hollywood producer wanted Arnold Schoenberg to compose incidental music for the movie version of Pearl Buck's novel *The Good Earth*. To get Mr. Schoenberg interested, the producer described a scene—a storm rages, an earthquake occurs, and in the middle of all this, the character Oo-lan gives birth. After the very vivid description, Mr. Schoenberg asked, "With so much going on, what do you need music for?"[193]

Names

• Actress Jennifer Love Hewitt began performing at age five. She turned up missing as her family was eating at a dining club, so her mother went looking for her. She found the five-year-old Love on a baby grand piano, singing "Help Me Make It Through the Night" to the diners. Of course, "Love" is an unusual name. She is named after a beautiful woman—her mother's best friend in college. Love says that her mother's best friend is actually very little like her. The best friend was 5-feet-11, with very long blonde hair and an hourglass figure. In contrast, Love is around 5-feet-3, with brown hair and, she says, "half an hourglass figure." With a name like Love, she should be a natural in the romance department, right? Not quite. Everyone has to learn the romance stuff as they go along in life. Her first on-screen kiss occurred when she was 14 years old—and had not had a real kiss yet. Her first attempt at an onscreen kiss resulted in the director ordering her and her kissing co-star to practice for a while before they attempted a second kiss for the cameras.[194]

• As a very young actress, Eliza Dushku worked with Arnold Schwarzenegger in the movie *True Lies*. She had never really planned to act, and her mother was not even close to being a stage mother, so they were learning what to do little by little, and lots of people were giving them lots of advice, including this: "Your kid has a funny name, Judy—you should think about changing it." Mr. Schwarzenegger, however, said, "Eliza, Judy, trust me, keep her name, people will learn it, take it from me."[195]

• Robert Towne wrote the screenplays for such classic movies as *Chinatown* and *The Last Detail*. His paternal grandfather had worked as a tanner in Minneapolis, Minnesota, but left because of the cold winters and came to California. In San Pedro, he opened a women's clothing store that was named the Towne Smart Shop, and when people started calling him Mr. Towne, he began to use "Towne" as his surname and passed the name down to his descendants.[196]

• The name of Spike Lee's film company is Forty Acres and a Mule Filmworks, because former slaves were promised 40 acres and a mule after the Civil War, but they never got what the government had promised. The name of his production company reminds Mr. Lee to rely on himself, not on the promises of other people.[197]

Parties

• In the mid-1960s, Dean Martin and his wife gave a black-tie anniversary party. Lots of people, including Frank Sinatra and other buddies and neighbors, came and enjoyed themselves, but at a little past 11 p.m. some police cars arrived and ordered everyone to be quiet. Mr. Sinatra was upset, and he asked a police officer to name the person who had called to complain. The police officer answered, "I'm not really at liberty to say," but eventually he admitted that the call had come from inside the house. Mr. Sinatra then went to Mr. Martin's bedroom, where he discovered the host of the party in pajamas and in bed, watching the evening news. Mr. Sinatra asked, "Did you call the cops on your own party?" Mr. Martin replied, "Hey, they ate, they drank. Let them go home. I gotta get up in the morning." Mr. Sinatra said, admiringly, "You are one crazy bast*rd." By the way, Mr. Martin was a member of Mr. Sinatra's rat pack, but on his own terms. When he felt like partying, he partied. When he felt like going to bed early so he could play golf in the morning, he went to bed early. Once, before his married days, Mr. Martin felt like going to bed early, but when he did, he discovered that Mr. Sinatra had paid a working girl $1,000 to be naked in Mr. Martin's bed. Mr. Martin wasn't interested, so he paid her $2,000 to go back to Mr. Sinatra and tell him that he was fabulous in bed. On another occasion, Mr. Sinatra got into a fight while in a hotel room where Mr. Martin was watching TV. Mr. Martin said, "Hey, can you guys fight a little to the left? I'm having trouble seeing the picture."[198]

• Rock star Rod Stewart went out with movie star Britt Ekland for a while, broke up with her, and then started going out with Alana Hamilton. Somehow, all three ended up at the same New Year's Eve party. Things were not pleasant between Britt and Alana, Rod was ill at ease, and at one point Britt started kissing Rod and would not stop kissing him. Alana let the kissing go on for a while, then, fed up, she poured her champagne down Britt's neck. Problem solved.[199]

Chapter 5: From Practical Jokes to Work

Practical Jokes

• Lynn Collins played Kayla Silverfox, the love interest of Wolverine in the 2009 action film *X-Men Origins: Wolverine*. Work on the movie started immediately. She says, "When I got the job, within 72 hours, I was on a cliff in my underwear kissing Hugh Jackman in New Zealand. I had no time to prepare." One "problem" arose during filming: Mr. Jackson told her that her outfits weren't skimpy enough to appeal to Wolverine. Ms. Collins responded, "[Expletive deleted.] OK. Whatever." Mr. Jackman then told her, "So, we found something for you. We put it in your trailer. Can you please try it on?" Ms. Collins found the new outfit—it was a definitely skimpy silver Spandex dress that did NOT cover the essentials that a dress usually covers. She put on the dress, and with some creative adjusting got it to cover the essentials, but when she opened the door to her trailer and peeked out, Mr. Jackman and lots of other people laughed at her. Mr. Jackman then said, "April Fool's." Mr. Jackman liked her response to the practical joke: "I love that you put it on and didn't slap me in the face."[200]

• We think of Paul Muni as a serious actor who undertook serious roles, winning an Oscar as Best Actor for playing the lead role in *The Story of Louis Pasteur*, but he was also a master of the put-on. He was born in what is now Ukraine, and when he was in his 30s, he became an American citizen by passing a test that asked questions about American history and politics. At the beginning of the test, he spoke with a heavy accent and looked puzzled by the questions he was being asked, but as the test continued he lost his accent and boldly answered the questions. When he answered the final question, he spoke with no accent at all, and then he told his examiner, "Your honor, it's remarkable. Now that you've made me a citizen, I can speak perfectly!"[201]

• Paul Newman and Robert Redford starred together in *Butch Cassidy and the Sundance Kid* and *The Sting*, and they were friends.

As a joke birthday present, Mr. Redford sent Mr. Newman a totally demolished Porsche. Mr. Newman had the car compacted into a 1-foot metal cube and then had it placed in Mr. Redford's living room—like a piece of sculpture. Mr. Newman enjoyed driving racecars, and he once had the logo of his racing competitor Bob Tullius painted upside down on a garbage truck and then driven around the racecourse. Mr. Tullius got back at Mr. Newman by persuading a couple of Georgia police officers to pull Mr. Newman over and threaten to detain him because of his crime of "impersonating an actor."[202]

• In a 2002 interview for *Esquire*, Cameron Diaz spoke about a notable practical joke that she played on unsuspecting guests at her home. She has a device that emits fart noises, and whenever a guest sits on a certain cushion located directly over the device, she uses a remote control to activate the device. Ms. Diaz says, "It's the best. It's like drugs. The first time you do it to somebody who's not expecting it—man, it's just the greatest high!" Unfortunately, the joke does have a drawback: "But you can never get away with it twice, so you have to move on to the next person."[203]

• As the male (and female) lead in *Tootsie*, Dustin Hoffman exhibited excellent acting. One day, Mr. Hoffman was dressed and in make-up as the character Dorothy Michaels, and he saw Jon Voight, with whom he had co-starred in *Midnight Cowboy*. "Dorothy" spoke to Mr. Voight, even complimenting him on his performance in *Midnight Cowboy*. Mr. Voight did not recognize that "Dorothy" was Mr. Hoffman.[204]

• Comedian Rich Hall used to have fun in New York City. He would take an old movie camera with him, stand on a street corner, wait for curious passersby to gather around, then say that he needed their help to finish making a low-budget horror movie. After he had passed out the scripts, people ran screaming on the sidewalks of New York.[205]

Problem-Solving

• In 1951, Barbara Stanwyck made the movie *To Please a Lady* with Clark Gable. The stars were going to stay at a good hotel in Indianapolis, Indiana, and when a business manager telephoned Barbara to ask her what arrangements she wanted, she informed him that she wanted a bedroom and bath, and a bedroom and a bath for her black maid, Harriet, and a sitting room in between the two bedrooms and baths. The business manager told her that Harriet could stay at a good hotel for blacks, but Harriet could not stay at their hotel. Barbara refused to compromise; she knew what she wanted and she told the business manager to make the arrangements that she wanted. Later, the producer telephoned Barbara to advise that she compromise and let Harriet stay at the "best colored hotel in Indianapolis." She told the producer, "I'll tell you what you can do to solve the whole thing. You make a reservation at the best colored hotel in Indianapolis for two bedrooms and baths and a sitting room between, and that's where I'll stay with Harriet." The producer told her, "Barbara, you can't do that!" Barbara replied, "The h*ll I can't!" Eventually, Barbara—and Harriet—stayed at the same hotel that the other movie stars were staying at.[206]

• Good deeds include helping celebrity friends get a little privacy. George Clooney once was able to give his friends Angelina Jolie and Brad Pitt a little privacy. Rumors spread that Mr. Pitt and Ms. Jolie were going to be married at Mr. Clooney's Italian home, Mr. Clooney rented hundreds of tables he did not need so that the rumor would be perpetuated and the paparazzi would go to his Italian home instead of to wherever Mr. Pitt and Ms. Jolie were. Speaking of rumors, before making the movie *Bridget Jones's Diary*, Renee Zellweger dated Jim Carrey, with whom she had starred in *Me, Myself & Irene*. When she walked on the set of *Bridget Jones's Diary* one day, she was applauded because everyone had heard that she had accepted a proposal from Mr. Carrey the night before. However, Ms. Zellweger was asleep at the time the proposal was supposed to have taken place. She was surprised that anyone was able to think that they had become engaged; after all, she points out, "I'd only been dating him a couple of months."[207]

• People who make low-budget movies have to be problem-solvers. For example, the critically acclaimed film *Crossover Dreams* was mostly filmed in a neighborhood in New York City. Often, people in the neighborhood would make meals for the filmmakers. To get apartments to film in, the crew used to paint those apartments in return. The actors mostly provided their own costumes. Unfortunately, the van in which the costumes were kept was stolen. A leather jacket worn by star Reubén Blades' character was among the items stolen; he replaced it at his own cost. Due to money problems, it took two years for the filming to be done. Mr. Blades had a mustache when he began acting in the film. Much later, when he returned to shoot the final scenes, he had shaved it off, so he had to wear a fake mustache.[208]

• Hollywood screenwriter Ben Hecht found it hard to do his job because he kept being interrupted and forced to attend story conferences with Sam Goldwyn. To solve his problem, he convinced Mr. Goldwyn to hire a collaborator for him, and he picked out Charles Lederer to work with. Thereafter, when Mr. Goldwyn called Mr. Hecht to a story conference, Mr. Hecht told Mr. Lederer exactly what to do—Mr. Lederer was to stretch out on a sofa in the conference room and go to sleep. This unnerved Mr. Goldwyn, but Mr. Hecht pointed out that under union rules, his collaborator had to attend story conferences with him. Soon, Mr. Goldwyn stopped forcing Mr. Hecht to attend story conferences, and Mr. Hecht was able to get some writing done.[209]

• In *Snow Angels*, directed by David Gordon Green, many interesting moments occur when Kate Beckinsale and Sam Rockwell act with three-year-old Gracie Hudson. During the making of the movie, Ms. Beckinsale and Mr. Rockwell were Gracie's "Pretend Mommy" and "Pretend Daddy." Mr. Green states, "Everybody always says, 'Don't work with animals and kids,' but those are the two greatest things." Gracie, of course, didn't understand about cameras and saying lines, so almost everything she said and did was unscripted. The exception: At one point, Mr. Green wanted her to say, "Can I play outside?" Mr. Green says, "That was the only thing that I needed her to say in the whole movie, and for that I had to give her Skittles."[210]

• For a while, actor Johnny Depp was engaged to actress Winona Ryder. In fact, for a while, Mr. Depp was engaged to so many women sequentially that a California bumper sticker stated, "Honk if you've never been engaged to Johnny Depp." The relationship was serious while it lasted, and Mr. Depp got a tattoo that stated, "Winona Forever." Ms. Ryder was present when he got the tattoo, although she was squeamish because she had never seen anyone get a tattoo before. Afterward, she kept asking him to raise the bandage so she could look at it. She said, "I was thrilled when he got the tattoo. Wouldn't any woman be?" Unfortunately, the relationship didn't last, so Mr. Depp got the tattoo changed to "Wino Forever."[211]

• In the 1930s, actors sometimes endorsed products, and they were promised one of whatever product they endorsed. However, very seldom did they get one of that product—either the product was not delivered, or someone stole the product before it reached the actor. Film actress Paulette Goddard learned quickly. She endorsed a large console radio, and after the advertisement photograph was taken, she said that she would take the radio now. The advertising man said, "You can't have this one. We have to shoot it with some other actresses." Ms. Goddard said, "I'm taking it now. Open the doors, boys." The "boys" opened the doors, revealing a truck waiting outside. Ms. Goddard got her radio.[212]

• Being a gorilla imitator can be a harrowing occupation, as during the filming of the Marx Brothers' *A Day at the Circus* an actor portraying the gorilla fainted twice because the owner of the gorilla skin refused to allow ventilation holes to be pierced in it because it was so valuable. However, one day the owner of the gorilla skin noticed something strange—the actor had been inside the gorilla skin for three hours and hadn't fainted yet (normally, anyone wearing the gorilla skin fainted after two hours). Investigating, he discovered that the actor had taken an icepick and made several unauthorized ventilation holes in the skin.[213]

• Dr. Joseph Goebbels, Minister of Propaganda for the Nazis, wanted Fritz Lang, the director of *Metropolis*, to join the Nazi effort and was willing to overlook Mr. Lang's maternal Jewish ancestors. Mr. Lang said that he would give Dr. Goebbels his answer within 24 hours, but that night he sneaked abroad a night train to Paris, carrying some money and jewelry with him. In his compartment, he hid the money under the carpet, and he taped the jewelry to some pipes in the bathroom. Only after crossing the border into France did he feel safe enough to retrieve his money and jewelry.[214]

• What are the anti-aging secrets of top movie stars? How is an aging movie star able to act credibly in an action movie? Of course, diet and exercise help, although tricks can help, too. For example, wrinkles in close-ups can be eliminated through technology after the film has been shot. In addition, hemorrhoid cream can work well for short periods of time, according to award-winning make-up artist Daniel Phillips. An aging star can put hemorrhoid cream on the bags under his eyes, and for a couple of hours the skin will tighten—long enough to shoot some close-ups.[215]

• While filming *Some Like It Hot*, Marilyn Monroe frequently had trouble remembering even the simplest lines. For example, in one scene she was supposed to open a drawer and say, "Where's the bourbon?" However, she blew the line in take after take. Therefore, director Billy Wilder ordered that the line be pasted in the drawer so she could read it. In the very next take, Ms. Monroe opened the wrong drawer—so Mr. Wilder ordered that the line be pasted in *every* drawer.[216]

• Producer-director Ismail Merchant (*Howards End, The Remains of the Day*) was often able to get very nice locations for his movies with very little expense. He once donned robes and posed as the Maharajah of Jodhpur as he walked into the Trianon Palace Hotel in Versailles. His crew carried in camera equipment as they pretended to be the Maharajah's entourage. Once all the equipment was inside the hotel, they began filming.[217]

• Actress Paula Raymond, star of *The Beast from 20,000 Fathoms*, became unhappy at Columbia, so she used a novel way of getting out of her contract—she ate her way out. When Columbia executives saw how plumb she was getting, they were happy to let her go.[218]

• Edward G. Robinson was a classic gangster in the movies, but he winced whenever he shot a gun. Once, director Mervyn Le Roy was forced to tell a makeup man to tape Robinson's eyelids open for each shooting scene in a movie.[219]

Screenwriters

• First-time filmmaker Marc Webb did not want to direct a romantic comedy—until he saw the screenplay for *(500) Days of Summer*, written by Scott Neustadter and Michael H. Weber. The first few lines were these: "Any resemblance to people living or dead is purely accidental. Especially Jenny Beckman. Bitch." "I liked that," Mr. Webb says. "It's fun, and it says, this movie is going to be a little bit different. You might have to engage a little more." The film was a hit and may someday be regarded as a classic—critic Roger Ebert gave it the top-rated 4 stars. Mr. Webb himself says, "I don't think this is a profoundly probing movie, but it's a simple movie that speaks a little bit of the truth, and just dances with reality and is fun."[220]

• Screenwriter Dan Berendsen writes movies for the Disney Channel; his work includes *The Cheetah Girls: One World*, *Twitches*, and *Wizards of Waverly Place: The Movie*. He actually started out as an insurance underwriter, but says, "After five years I thought I wanted to kill myself." Therefore, he researched business schools, but came across an article about the graduate screenwriting program at the University of Southern California. He applied and became one of the 15 people accepted out of approximately 2,000 applicants. He sold his house, moved to Southern California, and wrote. Today, when he signs his autograph for a young person, he adds, "Follow your dreams."[221]

Sex

• At one time actress Joan Collins supposedly had an affair with director and producer George Englund, but she cheated on him with a Dominican Republic dictator's son, who bought her a diamond necklace—something that made Mr. Englund jealous. However, Ms. Collins found a way to both keep the necklace and to stop Mr. Englund from being jealous. She had a cheap copy of the necklace made, then to show Mr. Englund that she loved him and only him, she threw the cheap imitation necklace, which he thought was the valuable real necklace, into the Pacific Ocean.[222]

• Gerard Butler has played a lot of macho roles, including that of King Leonides in the beefcake movie *300*, which featured great abdominals. This has apparently inspired a lot of lust (or satire) in his fans, as shown by the names of the groups of his fans on Facebook: "Gerard Butler Is My Husband—He Just Doesn't Know It Yet," "Gerard Butler Can Impregnate By Touch Alone," "Gerard Butler Can Make Even Physical Deformity Sexy" (he had the title role in *Phantom of the Opera*), "Please Have Your Way With My Naked Body, Gerard Butler," and "Gerard, I Want to Touch Your Butler."[223]

• Science-fiction author Harlan Ellison once briefly worked as a writer at Disney. Why briefly? On his first day of work, while taking a break in the cafeteria, he told his fellow workers about his ideas for an X-rated Disney cartoon, even going so far as to act out the scenes. His fellow employees were amused, but the bosses watching him from a distance were not amused. When he returned to his desk, he found a pink slip waiting for him. Journalist Andrew Osmond identifies the moral of this story: "Don't mess with the Mouse."[224]

Success

• Sometimes, achieving great success at a young age can lead to the problem of continually being asked about your early work despite all the good work you have done since then. One day, Orson Welles and Norman Mailer were having dinner when Mr. Mailer asked Mr. Welles a question about *Citizen Kane*, which Mr. Wells had created at age 25. Mr. Welles groaned and said, "Oh, Norman, not *Citizen Kane*." At first, Mr. Mailer was surprised, but then he realized what was the problem and said, mentioning his own youthful world-class work of art, "Mmm, yeah—it's like me and *The Naked and the Dead*." Other people also realized the burden that very great and very early success can have on a person. After seeing *Citizen Kane*, impresario Billy Rose told Mr. Welles, "Quit, kid—you'll never top it."[225]

• Actor Will Smith is known as a rapper, TV star, and movie star. He is also known for his ears, and he says that when he was a kid, he resembled Alfred E. Newman, the funny-looking character who graces the covers of *Mad* magazine. In fact, one of young Will's friends told him that he "looked like a car with the doors open." Today, as a major film star, Will knows exactly where to give the credit for his success: "It's the ears! Americans have an ear fetish. Absolutely. Americans love people with big ears—Mickey Mouse, Goofy, Ross Perot. America loves ears."[226]

Telegrams

• While Peter Ustinov was playing Nero in *Quo Vadis*, he frequently sent telegrams to VIPs in Hollywood, pointing out historical inaccuracies in the script and signing his name as "Nero Ustinov." In one telegram, he made the point that he was 32 years old and playing a man who had died at age 30. To his delight, Mr. Ustinov received this telegram from Hollywood: "TO EMPEROR NERO USTINOV, ROME. HISTORICAL RESEARCH PROVES THAT YOU REALLY ARE DEAD. IN VIEW OF THIS SAD DECEASE WE WOULD BE OBLIGED IF YOUR IMPERIAL MAJESTY WOULD REFRAIN FROM REWRITING THE SCRIPT."[227]

• When Ingrid Bergman arrived in Hollywood her first time, she sent fellow Swedish actress Greta Garbo—who desired privacy—some flowers and an invitation to have dinner and spend time together. Ms. Garbo accepted the invitation by telegram—three months later, when Ms. Bergman was leaving Hollywood. Ms. Bergman told George Cukor about Ms. Garbo's odd behavior. Mr. Cukor was friendly with Ms. Garbo, and he told Ms. Bergman, "Of course, Greta wouldn't have sent the telegram unless she was sure you were leaving."[228]

• Actor Cary Grant was capable of wit. He once gave a reporter permission to misquote him. Why would he do such a thing? He explained, "I improve in misquotation." And a magazine once sent him a telegram that asked, "HOW OLD CARY GRANT?" He replied with this telegram: "OLD CARY GRANT FINE. HOW YOU?"[229]

• Actress Gloria Swanson was quite the prima donna. In 1925, she returned to the United States after visiting France and marrying a titled Frenchman. On her American return, she telegraphed director Cecil B. DeMille, "AM ARRIVING WITH THE MARQUIS TOMORROW. PLEASE ARRANGE OVATION."[230]

Thanksgiving

• In 1939, May Wale Brown left Austria to come to New York City to be with her two brothers. She arrived on Thanksgiving Day, and of course the big Macy's Thanksgiving Day Parade was being held. Her brothers, who loved to tease her, told her that they had arranged the parade in order to welcome her to America. (By the way, Ms. Brown later became a Hollywood script supervisor.)[231]

War

• Mel Brooks, creator of such movies as *The Producers* and *Young Frankenstein*, enlisted in the United States Army in World War II and fought in the Battle of the Bulge. Once, the Germans rigged up a public address system and used it to broadcast Nazi propaganda to the Allies. Mr. Brooks retaliated by using the Allied PA system to broadcast his own version of Allied propaganda to the Nazis. Mr. Brooks' version of Allied propaganda included a rousing rendition of Al Jolson's hit "Toot Toot Tootsie Goodbye."[232]

• Controversial film director John Waters got out of being drafted during the Vietnam War by checking a number of boxes (including "gay") on a form and by weighing 129 pounds at a time when the minimum weight for a draftee was 130 pounds. He was classified 1Y, along with singer Iggy Pop, who had a very heavy illegal drug habit. When the Gulf War broke out, Iggy asked John, "Do you think they'll call us?" John answered that they would be called only after all the hairdressers had been called.[233]

• Drama critic George Oppenheimer was inducted into the Air Force, where he was a part of its Motion Picture Unit. As part of his physical, he gave a urine sample, which was picked up by a star-struck private, who put it on a tray and then pointed to another bottle on the tray and said with awe, "Cary Grant."[234]

Work

• Henry Lehrman, an actor, director, and producer, broke into show business with enthusiasm in the days of the silent movies. He thought that Hollywood filmmakers would be impressed by a French accent because of the movie success of the French company Pathé. Therefore, he showed up in Hollywood with a phony French accent that impressed no one. However, D.W. Griffith was shooting a scene in which a house burned, so Mr. Lehrman ran up the stairs of the burning building, and then he jumped out of a second-story window. Unfortunately, the cameraman had not filmed this exciting event. No problem. Mr. Lehrman ran up the stairs of the burning building a second time, and then he jumped out of a second-story window a second time. This time, the cameraman managed to film the exciting event, and Mr. Lehrman was on his way to a career in the movies.[235]

• Being an actor can be an insecure experience, as actors frequently worry about whether they will ever find another acting job. Alan Arkin tells a story about the great actor George C. Scott. One month after Mr. Scott had won an Oscar for Best Actor for his title role in *Patton*, a good friend of his visited him and heard him yelling. He was yelling for joy, screaming, "I got a job! I got a job!" Mr. Arkin makes the important point, "So most [actors] never get over that sense of never working again. It's a precarious life." Of course, Mr. Arkin tries to get quality jobs, although compromise can be a necessity: "I just want good material. But part of taking a role is your bank account. If you haven't worked in six months and the cupboard is bare, then your sights get lowered a bit out of necessity."[236]

• Early in the career of celebrity photographer Richard Young, he got a tip about where actor Ryan O'Neal was staying. Mr. O'Neal came out of the hotel and got into a car, and Mr. Young followed him in a taxi. Luckily, Mr. Young got a few shots of Mr. O'Neal before he went into a store. When Mr. O'Neal came out of the store, Mr. Young asked him, "Look, I just want a few shots. Can you pose up?" Mr. O'Neal was willing. He replied, "Sure, you guys really do work hard!" The two men did make an agreement: Once Mr. Young had got his shot, he would leave Mr. O'Neal alone. Mr. Young says, "That's exactly what I did."[237]

• Movie actress Raquel Welch, a USAmerican, has traveled widely, and one thing that she has learned from her travels is that Europeans often have an attitude toward certain kinds of work that is much different from the attitude that Americans have. For example, in the United States being a waiter is sometimes considered a menial job, but a European waiter often treats his work as an art form. The same is true of different kinds of craftsmen and -women. Ms. Welch points out, "All the things that people in this country consider menial and unfulfilling, people there are making an art out of."[238]

• Movie jobs are sometimes strange. For example, the movie *Desert Hearts*, about a lesbian relationship with a happy ending, required a spritzer. The movie has an important love scene between the main lesbian characters, and director Donna Deitch, who did the spritzing herself (because she didn't want too many people present during the filming of the scene), points out that the spritzer is "the person who in all love scenes or fight scenes, there's always somebody around who's gotta spritz them, 'cause you gotta have that sweat, some little bit of sweat."[239]

• Lon Chaney, Sr., aka the Man with a Thousand Faces, worked hard in his early days in movies. He sat in a room (called the bullpen) with many other bit-part actors. At times during a day, a director would come along and say something like "I need a college boy. Can anybody here play a college boy?" or "I need a Chinese man. Can anybody here play a Chinese man?" Whatever the director asked for, Mr. Chaney would say, "Yeah, I can play that." In this way, he made appearances in three or four movies each working day.[240]

• Mack Sennett made a lot of comedies in the silent-film days, including the famous Keystone Cops comedies. Mr. Sennett liked to keep an eye on his employees, so he had a tower built in the middle of his movie studio. That way, he could look out and see what everyone was doing. Mr. Sennett also loved taking baths, so he had a huge marble bathtub built in the tower. When he wasn't spying on his employees or doing real work such as planning a comedy, he was often either taking a bath or getting a massage.[241]

• Frequently, movie actors make a lot of money one year and not much money the next year. B movie actor Bruce Campbell once applied for a job as a security guard. The employment officer looked over his application, then said, "It says here, Mr. Campbell, that you made $125,000 last year. Is that true?" It was true, so he asked why Mr. Campbell was applying for a job as a security guard after making so much money. Mr. Campbell replied, "That was last year."[242]

• French comic filmmaker Jacques Tati carefully observed people and things, as they gave him ideas with which to work. Before creating his movie *Traffic*, he went to a highway and observed. One of the things he noticed was that many people driving away on holiday do not look happy. He also noticed a car in which was a dog that stared at a field that the dog could have played in. (I highly recommend his *M. Hulot's Holiday*, which doesn't need dialogue.)[243]

• Bob Hope made some very good movies and some very bad movies during his career. One of his very bad movies was a short titled *Going Spanish* which he made early in his career. Mr. Hope joked to columnist Walter Winchell about how bad the movie was: "When they catch [bank robber] John Dillinger, they're going to make him sit through it twice." Mr. Winchell printed the joke in his column, and Mr. Hope's movie company fired him.[244]

• English comedian Terry-Thomas was appearing in *The Brass Monkey* with actress Carole Landis, when the director began to worry about getting the movie finished quickly. The director asked Ms. Landis, "Let's get this thing in the can. Can we work faster?" Ms. Landis replied, "Not unless you can print on the film, 'Sorry, folks, about the poor quality, but we had to do it in a hurry.'"[245]

• At the premiere of the eccentric movie *Sylvia Scarlett*, audience reaction was so poor that director George Cukor and star Katherine Hepburn told producer Pandro Berman that they would make another movie for him for free. Mr. Berman turned them down, saying, "I don't want either of you ever to work for me again."[246]

• Buster Keaton was a hard-working comedian. Garry Moore once asked Buster how he was able to perform his pratfalls, and Buster said, "I'll show you." Then he showed Mr. Moore the bruises on his body. Mr. Moore later said, "So that's how he did it—*it hurt*—but you had to care enough not to care."[247]

• As you would expect, controversial filmmaker John Waters has long been outspoken. When he was young, he worked for three days in a unisex clothing store. Women would try on clothing and ask him,

"Do I look fat in this?" He would reply, "Yes." Perhaps unnecessarily, Mr. Waters says, "I was fired."[248]

• Spencer Tracy regarded making movies as a job. Once, he was working with a director who regarded making movies as an art. After listening to the director expound the symbolism in a scene for awhile, Mr. Tracy said, "I'm too tired and old and rich for all this, so let's do the scene."[249]

• Charlie Chaplin came to the United States as a member of a traveling comedy company: the Fred Karno Pantomime Troupe. As the boat sailed into the harbor, Mr. Chaplin stood up and proclaimed, "America, I am going to conquer you!" He did.[250]

Appendix A: Bibliography

Adams, Joey. *The God Bit*. Boston, MA: G.K. Hall & Co., 1975.

Bernotas, Bob. *Spike Lee: Filmmaker*. Hillside, NJ: Enslow Publications, Inc., 1993.

Bogdanovich, Peter. *Peter Bogdanovich's Movie of the Week*. New York: Ballantine Books, 1999.

Brandon, Karen. *Arnold Schwarzenegger*. San Diego, CA: Lucent Books, 2004.

Briggs, Joe Bob. *Profoundly Disturbing: Shocking Movies That Changed History!* New York: Universe Books, 2003.

Brown, David. *Star Billing: Tell-Tale Trivia from Hollywood*. London: Weidenfeld and Nicolson, Limited, 1985.

Brown, May Wale. *Reel Life on Hollywood Movie Sets*. Riverside, CA: Ariadne Press, 1995.

Bryant, Gay, and Bockris-Wylie. *How I Learned to Like Myself*. New York: Warner Paperback Library, 1975.

Campbell, Bruce. *If Chins Could Kill: Confessions of a B Movie Actor*. New York: Thomas Dunne Books, 2001.

Carradine, David. *The Kill Bill Diary*. New York: HarperCollins Publishers, 2006.

Cox, Stephen. *The Munchkins Remember*: The Wizard of Oz *and Beyond*. New York: E.P. Dutton, 1989.

Damon, Duane. *Headin' for Better Times*. Minneapolis, MN. Lerner Publications Company, 2002.

Dean, Tanya. *Theodor Geisel (Dr. Seuss)*. New York: Chelsea House Publishers, 2002.

Duncan, Kenn. *Divas: The Fabulous Photography of Kenn Duncan*. Text by Stephen M. Silverman. New York: Universe Publishing, 2008.

DuPont, Lonnie Hull. *Mike Myers*. Philadelphia, PA: Chelsea House Publishers, 2000.

Edelson, Edward. *Funny Men of the Movies*. New York: Pocket Books, 1976.

Edelson, Edward. *Great Kids of the Movies*. Garden City, NY: Doubleday and Co., Inc., 1979.

Edelson, Paula. *Cuba Gooding, Jr*. Philadelphia, PA: Chelsea House Publishers, 2000.

Eichenbaum, Rose. *Masters of Movement: Portraits of America's Great Choreographers*. Washington, D.C.: Smithsonian Books, 2004.

Engstead, John. *Star Shots: Fifty Years of Pictures and Stories by One of Hollywood's Greatest Photographers*. New York: E.P. Dutton, 1978.

Ferrer, Sean Hepburn. *Audrey Hepburn: An Elegant Spirit*. New York: Atria Books, 2003.

Fox, Patty. *Star Style: Hollywood Legends as Fashion Icons*. Santa Monica, CA: Angel City Press, Inc., 1995.

Franklin, Joe. *Up Late with Joe Franklin*. New York: Scribner, 1995.

Gallo, Hank. *Comedy Explosion: A New Generation*. Photographs by Ed Edahl. New York: Thunder's Mouth Press, 1991.

Garner, Joe. *Made You Laugh: the Funniest Moments in Radio, Television, Stand-up, and Movie Comedy*. Kansas City, MO: Andrews McMeel Publishing, 2004.

Garner, Joe. *Now Showing: Unforgettable Moments from the Movies*. Kansas City, MO: Andrews McMeel Publishing, 2003.

Gilliatt, Penelope. *Jacques Tati*. London: The Woburn Press, 1976.

Greene, Meg. *Will Smith*. Philadelphia, PA: Chelsea House Publishers, 2002.

Grody, Svetlana McLee, and Dorothy Daniels Lister. *Conversations With Choreographers*. Portsmouth, NH: Heinemann, 1996.

Gruen, John. *People Who Dance*. Pennington, NJ: Princeton Book Company, 1988.

Guttmacher, Peter. *Legendary Horror Films*. New York: MetroBooks, 1995.

Halliwell, Leslie. *The Filmgoer's Book of Quotes*. New Rochelle, NY: Arlington House Publishers, 1973.

Hay, Peter. *Movie Anecdotes*. New York: Oxford University Press, 1990.

Hecht, Andrew. *Hollywood Merry-Go-Round*. New York: Grosset and Dunlap, Publishers, 1947.

Hecht, Ben. *Charlie: The Improbable Life and Times of Charles MacArthur*. New York: Harper & Brothers, Publishers, 1957.

Hill, Anne E. *Cameron Diaz*. Philadelphia, PA: Chelsea House Publishers, 2000.

Hill, Anne E. *Sandra Bullock*. San Diego, CA: Lucent Books, 2001.

Isenberg, Barbara. *State of the Arts: California Artists Talk About Their Work*. Chicago, IL: Ivan R. Dee, 2000.

Ives, John G. *John Waters*. Photographs by F-Stop Fitzgerald. New York: Thunder's Mouth Press, 1992.

Jackson, Kathy Merlock, editor. *Walt Disney Conversations*. Jackson, Mississippi: University Press of Mississippi, 2006.

Johnstone, Nick. *Johnny Depp: The Illustrated Biography*. London: Carlton Books, Ltd., 2006.

Jones, Veda Boyd. *Ewan McGregor*. Philadelphia, PA: Chelsea House Publishers, 2000.

Karsh, Yousuf. *Karsh: A Biography in Images*. Boston, MA: MFA Publications, 2003.

Karsh, Yousuf. *Karsh: A Sixty-Year Retrospective*. Boston, MA: Little, Brown and Company, 1996.

Kline, Sally, editor. *George Lucas: Interviews*. Jackson, MS: University Press of Mississippi, 1999.

Lemmon, Chris. *A Twist of Lemmon: A Tribute to My Father*. Chapel Hill, NC: Algonquin Books of Chapel Hill, 2006.

Levant, Oscar. *A Smattering of Ignorance*. New York: Doubleday, Doran, and Co., 1940.

Linkletter, Art. *Women are My Favorite People*. Garden City, NY: Doubleday & Company, Inc., 1974.

Lynette, Rachel. *Angelina Jolie*. Detroit, MI: Lucent Books, 2007.

Lynette, Rachel. *Tim Burton: Filmmaker*. Farmington Hills, MI: KidHaven Press, 2007.

Maltin, Leonard. *The Great Movie Comedians: From Charlie Chaplin to Woody Allen*. New York: Crown Publishers, Inc., 1978.

Manchel, Frank. *The Box Office Clowns*. New York: Franklin Watts, 1979.

Manchel, Frank. *Yesterday's Clowns: The Rise of Film Comedy*. New York: Franklin Watts, Inc., 1973.

Marcovitz, Hal. *Will Hobbes*. Philadelphia, PA: Chelsea House Publishers, 2006.

Marton, Betty A. *Reubén Blades*. New York: Chelsea House Publishers, 1992.

Marx, Groucho. *Groucho and Me*. New York: Bernard Geis Associates, 1959.

Marx, Groucho. *Groucho Marx and Other Short Stories and Tall Tales*. Edited by Robert S. Bader. Boston, MA: Faber and Faber, 1996.

Marx, Maxine. *Growing Up with Chico*. New York: Limelight Editions, 1986.

McAvoy, Jim. *Tom Hanks*. Philadelphia, PA: Chelsea House Publishers, 2000.

McNeil, Legs, and Gillian McCain. *Please Kill Me: The Uncensored Oral History of Punk*. New York: Penguin Books, 1997.

Metil, Luana, and Jace Townsend. *The Story of Karate: From Buddhism to Bruce Lee*. Minneapolis, MN: Lerner Publications Company, 1995.

Meyer, Miriam Weiss, Project Editor. *Top Picks: People*. Pleasantville, NY: Reader's Digest Educational Division, 1977.

Miller, John, editor. *Legends: Women Who Have Changed the World*. Novato, CA: New World Books, 1998.

Nash, Bruce, and Allan Zullo. *The Hollywood Walk of Shame*. Compiled by Martha Moffett. Kansas City, MO: Andrews and McMeel, 1993.

Nerz, A. Ryan. *Jennifer Love Hewitt*. New York: Aladdin Paperbacks, 1998.

Netter, Susan. *Paul Newman and Joanne Woodward: An Unauthorized Biography.* London: Sphere Books, Ltd., 1989.

Oleksy, Walter. *Christopher Reeve.* San Diego, CA: Lucent Books, 2000.

Otfinoski, Steven. *Stan Lee: Comic Book Genius.* New York: Franklin Watts, 2007.

Parish, James Robert. *Denzel Washington: Actor.* New York: Ferguson, 2005.

Parla, Paul, and Charles P. Mitchell. *Screen Sirens Scream!* Jefferson, NC, and London: McFarland and Company, Inc., Publishers, 2000.

Pela, Robrt L. *Filthy: The Weird World of John Waters.* Los Angeles, CA: Alyson Books, 2002.

Powers, Tom. *Horror Movies.* Minneapolis, MN: Lerner Publications Company, 1989.

Powers, Tom. *Steven Spielberg: Master Storyteller.* Minneapolis, MN: Lerner Publications Company, 1997.

Primack, Ben, adapter and editor. *The Ben Hecht Show: Impolitic Observations from the Freest Thinker of 1950s Television.* Jefferson, NC: McFarland & Company, Inc., Publishers, 1993.

Richards, Dick, compiler. *The Wit of Peter Ustinov.* London: Leslie Frewin Publishers, Limited, 1969.

Rubin, Susan Goldman. *Steven Spielberg: Crazy for Movies.* New York: Harry N. Abrams, Inc., 2001.

Schickel, Richard. *Cary Grant: A Celebration.* Boston, MA: Little, Brown and Company, 1983.

Shields, Charles J. *I am Scout: The Biography of Harper Lee.* New York: Henry Holt and Company, 2008.

Slezak, Walter. *What Time's the Next Swan?* Garden City, NY: Doubleday and Co., Inc., 1962.

Smith, H. Allen. *Buskin' With H. Allen Smith.* New York: Trident Press, 1968.

Sobol, Donald J. *Encyclopedia Brown's Book of Wacky Cars.* New York: William Morrow and Company, Inc., 1987.

Sorel, Nancy Caldwell, and Edward Sorel. *First Encounters: A Book of Memorable Meetings.* New York: Alfred A. Knopf, 1994.

Stauffer, Stacey. *Leonardo DiCaprio.* Philadelphia, PA: Chelsea House Publishers, 1999.

Terry-Thomas, and Terry Daum. *Terry-Thomas ... Tells Tales.* London: Robson Books, 1990.

Topol, Chaim, compiler. *Topol's Treasury of Jewish Humor, Wit and Wisdom.* New York: Barricade Books, Inc., 1994.

Vilanch, Bruce. *Bruce! Adventures in the Skin Trade and Other Essays*. New York: Jeremy P. Tarcher/Putnam, 2000.

Wallach, Eli. *The Good, the Bad, and Me: In My Anecdotage*. Orlando, FL: Harcourt, Inc., 2005.

Waters, John. *Crackpot: The Obsessions of John Waters*. New York: Vintage Books, 1987.

Willson, Meredith. *And There I Stood With My Piccolo*. Westport, CT: Greenwood Press, Publishers, 1948.

Young, Richard. *Shooting Stars*. London: Metro Publishing, Ltd., 2004.

Zehme, Bill. *The Way You Wear Your Hat: Frank Sinatra and the Lost Art of Livin'*. New York: HarperCollinsPublishers, 1997.

Appendix B: About the Author

It was a dark and stormy night. Suddenly a cry rang out, and on a hot summer night in 1954, Josephine, wife of Carl Bruce, gave birth to a boy—me. Unfortunately, this young married couple allowed Reuben Saturday, Josephine's brother, to name their first-born. Reuben, aka "The Joker," decided that Bruce was a nice name, so he decided to name me Bruce Bruce. I have gone by my middle name—David—ever since.

Being named Bruce David Bruce hasn't been all bad. Bank tellers remember me very quickly, so I don't often have to show an ID. It can be fun in charades, also. When I was a counselor as a teenager at Camp Echoing Hills in Warsaw, Ohio, a fellow counselor gave the signs for "sounds like" and "two words," then she pointed to a bruise on her leg twice. Bruise Bruise? Oh, yeah, Bruce Bruce is the answer!

Uncle Reuben, by the way, gave me a haircut when I was in kindergarten. He cut my hair short and shaved a small bald spot on the back of my head. My mother wouldn't let me go to school until the bald spot grew out again.

Of all my brothers and sisters (six in all), I am the only transplant to Athens, Ohio. I was born in Newark, Ohio, and have lived all around Southeastern Ohio. However, I moved to Athens to go to Ohio University and have never left.

At Ohio U, I never could make up my mind whether to major in English or Philosophy, so I got a bachelor's degree with a double major in both areas, then I added a Master of Arts degree in English and a Master of Arts degree in Philosophy. Yes, I have my MAMA degree.

Currently, and for a long time to come (I eat fruits and veggies), I am spending my retirement writing books such as *Nadia Comaneci: Perfect 10*, *The Funniest People in Comedy*, *Homer's* Iliad: *A Retelling in Prose*, and *William Shakespeare's* Hamlet: *A Retelling in Prose*.

If all goes well, I will publish one or two books a year for the rest of my life. (On the other hand, a good way to make God laugh is to tell Her your plans.)

By the way, my sister Brenda Kennedy writes romances such as *A New Beginning* and *Shattered Dreams*.

Appendix C: Some Books by David Bruce

Anecdote Collections

250 Anecdotes About Opera
250 Anecdotes About Religion
250 Anecdotes About Religion: Volume 2
250 Music Anecdotes
Be a Work of Art: 250 Anecdotes and Stories
The Coolest People in Art: 250 Anecdotes
The Coolest People in the Arts: 250 Anecdotes
The Coolest People in Books: 250 Anecdotes
The Coolest People in Comedy: 250 Anecdotes
Create, Then Take a Break: 250 Anecdotes
Don't Fear the Reaper: 250 Anecdotes
The Funniest People in Art: 250 Anecdotes
The Funniest People in Books: 250 Anecdotes
The Funniest People in Books, Volume 2: 250 Anecdotes
The Funniest People in Books, Volume 3: 250 Anecdotes
The Funniest People in Comedy: 250 Anecdotes
The Funniest People in Dance: 250 Anecdotes
The Funniest People in Families: 250 Anecdotes
The Funniest People in Families, Volume 2: 250 Anecdotes
The Funniest People in Families, Volume 3: 250 Anecdotes
The Funniest People in Families, Volume 4: 250 Anecdotes
The Funniest People in Families, Volume 5: 250 Anecdotes
The Funniest People in Families, Volume 6: 250 Anecdotes
The Funniest People in Movies: 250 Anecdotes
The Funniest People in Music: 250 Anecdotes
The Funniest People in Music, Volume 2: 250 Anecdotes
The Funniest People in Music, Volume 3: 250 Anecdotes
The Funniest People in Neighborhoods: 250 Anecdotes
The Funniest People in Relationships: 250 Anecdotes
The Funniest People in Sports: 250 Anecdotes
The Funniest People in Sports, Volume 2: 250 Anecdotes
The Funniest People in Television and Radio: 250 Anecdotes
The Funniest People in Theater: 250 Anecdotes

The Funniest People Who Live Life: 250 Anecdotes
The Funniest People Who Live Life, Volume 2: 250 Anecdotes
The Kindest People Who Do Good Deeds, Volume 1: 250 Anecdotes
The Kindest People Who Do Good Deeds, Volume 2: 250 Anecdotes
Maximum Cool: 250 Anecdotes
The Most Interesting People in Movies: 250 Anecdotes
The Most Interesting People in Politics and History: 250 Anecdotes
The Most Interesting People in Politics and History, Volume 2: 250 Anecdotes
The Most Interesting People in Politics and History, Volume 3: 250 Anecdotes
The Most Interesting People in Religion: 250 Anecdotes
The Most Interesting People in Sports: 250 Anecdotes
The Most Interesting People Who Live Life: 250 Anecdotes
The Most Interesting People Who Live Life, Volume 2: 250 Anecdotes
Reality is Fabulous: 250 Anecdotes and Stories
Resist Psychic Death: 250 Anecdotes
Seize the Day: 250 Anecdotes and Stories

[1] Source: Barry Koltnow, "An Oscar winner and a teen actress delve into dark places." *The Orange County Register*. March 2008 <http://www.popmatters.com/pm/news/article/56425/an-oscar-winner-and-a-teen-actress-delve-into-dark-places/>.

[2] Source: Harvey Weinstein, "Anthony Minghella, my teacher, my friend." *The Times*. 10 April 2008 <http://entertainment.timesonline.co.uk/tol/arts_and_entertainment/film/article3714086.ece>.

[3] Source: Paula Edelson, *Cuba Gooding, Jr.*, pp. 67-69, 71.

[4] Source: Rachel Lynette, *Angelina Jolie*, p. 50.

[5] Source: Charles J. Shields, *I am Scout: The Biography of Harper Lee*, pp. 144, 172.

[6] Source: Edward Edelson, *Great Kids of the Movies*, pp. 11-12.

[7] Source: Roger Moore, "Chatting with first-time nominees Ellen Page, Ruby Dee and Marjane Satrapi." *Orlando Sentinel*. February 2008 <http://www.popmatters.com/pm/news/article/55320/chatting-with-first-time-nominees-ellen-page-ruby-dee-and-marjane-satrapi/>.

[8] Source: Bruce Nash and Allan Zullo, *The Hollywood Walk of Shame*, p. 101.

[9] Source: Judith Lewis, "Jodie Foster Discusses 'The Brave One.'" *LA Weekly*. 5 September 2007 <http://www.laweekly.com/general/features/jodie-foster-chaos-control/17151/>.

[10] Source: Matthew Sweet, "Snakes, slaves and seduction." *The Guardian*. 6 February 2008 <http://www.guardian.co.uk/g2/story/0,,2252998,00.html>.

[11] Source: Erik Himmelsbach, "Jeff Bridges: Iron Dude." 29 November 2007 <http://www.lacitybeat.com/article.php?id=6562&IssueNum=234>.

[12] Source: Jasper Rees, "And Kenneth makes three." *The Sunday Times*. 23 September 2007 <http://entertainment.timesonline.co.uk/tol/arts_and_entertainment/film/article2499835.ece>.

[13] Source: Cole Hadden, "Runaway train." *San Antonio Current*. 5 September 2007 <http://www.sacurrent.com/film/story.asp?id=67351>. Also: Glenn Sumi, "Laura Linney." *NOW Magazine*. 6-12 September 2007 <http://www.nowtoronto.com/issues/2007-09-06/cover_story.php>.

[14] Source: May Wale Brown, *Reel Life on Hollywood Movie Sets*, p. 212.

[15] Source: Simon Hattenstone, "A good loser." *The Guardian*. 27 October 2007 <http://www.guardian.co.uk/weekend/story/0,,2198806,00.html>.

[16] Source: Joseph V. Amodio, "Scottish actor Ewan McGregor is in big demand." *Newsday*. 31 January 2008 <http://www.popmatters.com/pm/news/article/53730/scottish-actor-ewan-mcgregor-is-in-big-demand/>.

[17] Source: Walter Slezak, *What Time's the Next Swan?*, p. 31.

[18] Source: James Bone, "Ewan McGregor on erotic thriller *Deception*." *The Times*. 12 April 2008 <http://entertainment.timesonline.co.uk/tol/arts_and_entertainment/film/article3707253.ece>.

[19] Source: Luana Metil and Jace Townsend, *The Story of Karate: From Buddhism to Bruce Lee*, p. 82.

[20] Source: Roger Moore, "Karen Allen is back where she belongs: in an Indiana Jones movie." *The Orlando Sentinel*. 19 May 2008 <http://www.popmatters.com/pm/news/article/58763/karen-allen-is-back-where-she-belongs-in-an-indiana-jones-movie/>.

[21] Source: Ray Pride, "Talking 'Married Life' with Ira Sachs and Chris Cooper." *Chicago Newcity*. 11 March 2008 <http://newcitychicago.com/chicago/7558.html>.

[22] Source: Peter Bogdanovich, *Peter Bogdanovich's Movie of the Week*, p. 159.

[23] Source: Barry Koltnow, "Jack of all trades: Nicholson stars as a dying man." *The Orange County Register*. 2 January 2008 <http://www.popmatters.com/pm/news/article/52623/jack-of-all-trades-nicholson-stars-as-a-dying-man/>.

[24] Source: Madeleine Marr, "Virginia Madsen keeping busy with 3 movies in the works." McClatchy Newspapers. 23 June 2008 <http://www.popmatters.com/pm/news/article/60087/virginia-madsen-keeping-busy-with-3-movies-in-the-works/>.

[25] Source: Geoffrey McNab, "Memories of a child star." *The Guardian*. 30 May 2008 <http://film.guardian.co.uk/interview/interviewpages/0,,2282728,00.html>.

[26] Source: John Carvill, "Celebrating Bogie." 18 September 2007 <http://www.popmatters.com/pm/features/article/47878/celebrating-bogie/>.

[27] Source: Yousuf Karsh, *Karsh: A Sixty-Year Retrospective*, p. 186.

[28] Source: Kevin Maher, "Me and Mr Jones: is John Hurt a villain?" *The Times*. 8 May 2008 <http://entertainment.timesonline.co.uk/tol/arts_and_entertainment/film/article3887343.ece>.

[29] Source: Roger Ebert, "Jarmusch shows 'the Money.'" 31 July 31 2005 <rogerebert.suntimes.com/apps/pbcs.dll/article?AID=/20050731/PEOPLE/507310301>.

[30] Source: Rachel Leibrock, "Dramatic turn: Ryan Reynolds steps away from being the funny guy." McClatchy Newspapers. 11 February 2008 <http://www.popmatters.com/pm/news/article/54667/dramatic-turn-ryan-reynolds-steps-away-from-being-the-funny-guy/>.

[31] Source: Chris Lemmon, *A Twist of Lemmon: A Tribute to My Father*, pp. 41-42.

[32] Source: Will Harris, "A Chat with Chris Lemmon, Author of 'A Twist of Lemmon: A Tribute to My Father.'" Bullz-eye.com. 23 July 2008 <http://www.bullz-eye.com/books/interviews/2008/chris_lemmon.htm>.

[33] Source: Yousuf Karsh, *Karsh: A Sixty-Year Retrospective*, p. 177.

[34] Source: Cary Darling, "'Harold & Kumar' make an encore appearance, at... Guantanamo Bay." McClatchy Newspapers. 18 April 2008 <http://www.popmatters.com/pm/news/article/57530/harold-kumar-make-an-encore-appearance-at-guantanamo-bay/>.

[35] Source: Barbara Ellen, "What lies beneath." *The Guardian*. 30 December 2007 <http://film.guardian.co.uk/interview/interviewpages/0,,2232184,00.html>.

[36] Source: Luaine Lee, "Angie Harmon plays Lily Tartikoff in Lifetime movie 'Living Proof.'" McClatchy-Tribune News Service. 14 October 2008 <http://www.popmatters.com/pm/article/64405/angie-harmon-plays-lily-tartikoff-in-lifetime-movie-living-proof/>.

[37] Source: Donald J. Sobol, *Encyclopedia Brown's Book of Wacky Cars*, pp. 15-16.

[38] Source: Donald Liebenson, "Paul Newman: No Autographs, Please." *Huffington Post*. 6 October 2008 <http://www.huffingtonpost.com/donald-liebenson/paul-newman-no-autographs_b_130997.html>.

[39] Source: Robrt L. Pela, *Filthy: The Weird World of John Waters*, p. 25. (Yes, "Robrt" is the correct spelling.)

[40] Source: Alan Scherstuhl, "Fox 4's Shawn Edwards isn't just a blurb whore." 3 April 2008 <http://news.pitch.com/2008-04-03/news/fox-4-s-shawn-edwards-isn-t-just-a-blurb-whore/>.

[41] Source: Louis Virtel, "13 Embarrassing Questions for Jackie Collins." *The Advocate*. 6 June 2008 <http://www.advocate.com/exclusive_detail_ektid55180.asp>.

[42] Source: David Carradine, *The Kill Bill Diary*, pp. 30-31.

[43] Source: Colin Covert, "Minnesota has another pair of hot moviemaking brothers in Drew and John Erick Dowdle." *Star Tribune* (Minneapolis, MN). 30 October 2008 <http://www.popmatters.com/pm/article/65109/minnesota-has-another-pair-of-hot-moviemaking-brothers-in-drew-and-john-eri/>.

[44] Source: Rick Bentley, "Dustin Hoffman is the voice of authority in 'Kung Fu Panda.'" McClatchy Newspapers. 5 June 2008 <http://www.popmatters.com/pm/news/article/59463/dustin-hoffman-is-the-voice-of-authority-in-kung-fu-panda/>.

[45] Source: Charles J. Shields, *I am Scout: The Biography of Harper Lee*, pp. 156-157, 167.

[46] Source: Rose Eichenbaum, *Masters of Movement: Portraits of America's Great Choreographers*, p. 10.

[47] Source: Stephen Armstrong, "The fun also rises for Steve Carell." *The Times*. 3 August 2008 <http://women.timesonline.co.uk/tol/life_and_style/women/celebrity/article4431330.ece>.

[48] Source: Tom Powers, *Horror Movies*, pp. 42-43.

[49] Source: Rachel Lynette, *Angelina Jolie*, p. 18.

[50] Source: "Brad Pitt: My Kids Are 'the Funniest People I've Ever Met.'" *Us Magazine*. 18 November 2008 <http://omg.yahoo.com/news/brad-pitt-my-kids-are-the-funniest-people-i-ve-ever-met/15550>.

[51] Source: Rachel Lynette, *Tim Burton: Filmmaker*, pp. 13-14.

[52] Source: Hal Marcovitz, *Will Hobbes*, p. 46.

[53] Source: Anne E. Hill, *Sandra Bullock*, p. 13.

[54] Source: Maxine Marx, *Growing Up with Chico*, pp. 65-66.

[55] Source: Emily Wilson, "Slay it again." *The Guardian*. 2 April 2007 <http://www.guardian.co.uk/g2/story/0,,2047890,00.html>.

[56] Source: Tom Powers, *Steven Spielberg: Master Storyteller*, p. 10.

[57] Source: Tanya Dean, *Theodor Geisel (Dr. Seuss)*, pp. 73, 96.

[58] Source: Stephen Cox, *The Munchkins Remember*, pp. 29-31.

[59] Source: Ben Primack, adapter and editor, *The Ben Hecht Show*, p. 128.

[60] Source: Legs McNeil and Gillian McCain, *Please Kill Me*, p. 91.

[61] Source: Rachel Cooke, "Turner's prize." *The Guardian*. 2 March 2008 <http://film.guardian.co.uk/interview/interviewpages/0,,2261367,00.html>.

[62] Source: Joel Stein, "Paparazzi avoidance behavior." *Los Angeles Times*. 16 May 2008 <http://www.latimes.com/news/opinion/commentary/la-oe-stein16-2008may16,0,542835.column>.

[63] Source: Greg Archer, "The Kid Stays in the Picture." *The Advocate*. 26 November 2008 <http://www.advocate.com/exclusive_detail_ektid66464.asp>.

[64] Source: Joel Stein, "Peter Principle of award shows." *Los Angeles Times*. 15 February 2008 <http://www.latimes.com/news/opinion/commentary/la-oe-stein15feb15,0,1384648.column>.

[65] Source: Joan Collins, "Bette Davis taught me to be a bitch." *The Times*. 27 March 2008 <http://entertainment.timesonline.co.uk/tol/arts_and_entertainment/film/article3626790.ece>.

[66] Source: Patty Fox, *Star Style: Hollywood Legends as Fashion Icons*, p. 27.

[67] Source: Francesco Vezzoli and Christopher Bollen, "Roman Polanski." *Interview Magazine*. Viewed 26 January 2009 <http://www.interviewmagazine.com/film/roman-polanski-/>.

[68] Source: Groucho Marx, *Groucho Marx and Other Short Stories and Tall Tales*, p. 41.

[69]Source: Hank Gallo, *Comedy Explosion: A New Generation*, p. 106.

[70] Source: Brian Juergens, "*The Adventures of Priscilla, Queen of the Desert*: Sand, Sequins and Song." 4 June 2007 <http://www.afterelton.com/movies/2007/6/priscillaqueenofthedesert>.

[71] Source: Tom Horgen, "Comics are leaping from page to screen." *Star Tribune* (Minneapolis, MN). 27 June 2008 <http://www.popmatters.com/pm/article/60265/comics-are-leaping-from-page-to-screen/>.

[72]Source: Joe Bob Briggs, *Profoundly Disturbing: Shocking Movies That Changed History!*, p. 161.

[73]Source: John Waters, *Crackpot: The Obsessions of John Waters*, p. 47.

[74]Source: Joe Garner, *Now Showing: Unforgettable Moments from the Movies*, pp. 36-37.

[75]Source: Peter Hay, *Movie Anecdotes*, p. 248.

[76]Source: Oscar Levant, *A Smattering of Ignorance*, pp. 79-80.

[77] Source: Kenn Duncan, *Divas: The Fabulous Photography of Kenn Duncan*, p. 188.

[78] Source: Joe Franklin, *Up Late with Joe Franklin*, pp. 41-42.

[79] Source: Giles Harvey, "This Gravity-Ridden World: A Review of *Conquest of the Useless: Reflections from the Making of* Fitzcarraldo by Werner Herzog." 20 September 2009 <http://www.powells.com/review/2009_09_20.html>. Published originally in the *Virginia Quarterly Review*.

[80] Source: Eli Wallach, *The Good, the Bad, and Me: In My Anecdotage*, p. 206.

[81]Source: Peter Hay, *Movie Anecdotes*, p. 278.

[82] Source: Joan Hackett, "Interesting Epitaph." <http://www.findagrave.com/cgi-bin/fg.cgi?page=gr&GSie=1&GRid=1447&>. Also: Jack Lemmon, "Interesting Epitaph." <http://www.findagrave.com/cgi-bin/fg.cgi?page=gr&GSie=1&GRid=22822&>.

[83] Source: Simon Hattenstone, "Laughter and loss." *The Guardian*. 6 September 2008 <http://www.guardian.co.uk/lifeandstyle/2008/sep/06/tsunami2004.worldcinema>.

[84] Source: Jason Solomons, "Interview with John Waters." *The Guardian*. 30 September 2007 <http://film.guardian.co.uk/features/featurepages/0,,2180140,00.html>.

[85] Source: Roger Moore, "Still larger than life, Francis Ford Coppola now thinks smaller." *The Orlando Sentinel*. 25 January 2008 <http://www.popmatters.com/pm/news/article/53506/still-larger-than-life-francis-ford-coppola-now-thinks-smaller/>.

[86] Source: Colin Covert, "John Waters talks (and talks) about his subversive career." 8 November 2007 <http://www.popmatters.com/pm/news/article/50712/john-waters-talks-and-talks-about-his-subversive-career/>. This article originally appeared in the *Star Tribune* (Minneapolis, MN).

[87] Source: Robert W. Butler, "In a new book dozens of luminaries tell tales of the brilliant, stubborn Robert Altman." McClatchy Newspapers. 7 October 2009 <http://www.popmatters.com/pm/article/112802-in-a-new-book-dozens-of-luminaries-tell-tales-of-the-brilliant-stubb/>.

[88] Source: Alan Yentob, "Herzog still follows the call of the wild." *The Times*. <http://entertainment.timesonline.co.uk/tol/arts_and_entertainment/film/article4212984.ece>.

[89] Source: Tom Powers, *Horror Movies*, p. 33.

[90] Source: Jim McAvoy, *Tom Hanks*, pp. 39-40.

[91] Source: Leslie Halliwell, *The Filmgoer's Book of Quotes*, p. 94.

[92] Source: Stephen Moss, "The late developer." *The Guardian*. 7 November 2007 <http://www.guardian.co.uk/g2/story/0,,2206338,00.html>.

[93] Source: David Hiltbrand, "Corbin Bernsen is loving every role, as Mom advised." *The Philadelphia Inquirer*. 18 July 2008 <http://www.popmatters.com/pm/article/61090/corbin-bernsen-is-loving-every-role-as-mom-advised/>.

[94] Source: Kathy Merlock Jackson, editor. *Walt Disney Conversations*, p. 9.

[95] Source: Rose Eichenbaum, *Masters of Movement: Portraits of America's Great Choreographers*, p. 171.

[96] Source: Gay Bryant and Bockris-Wylie, *How I Learned to Like Myself*, p. 74.

[97] Source: John Gruen, *People Who Dance*, p. 88.

[98] Source: Karen Brandon, *Arnold Schwarzenegger*, p. 17.

[99] Source: Chrissy Iley, "Not afraid of the dark." *The Guardian*. 25 September 2007 <http://www.guardian.co.uk/g2/story/0,,2176482,00.html>.

[100] Source: Robert Fulford, "Always settle scores at noon, And other lessons learned at the movies." *National Post*. 9 September 2008 <http://www.nationalpost.com/story-printer.html?id=36f969da-42fd-4a06-b10b-084f758d1765>.

[101] Source: Froma Harrop, "Newman Embraced Ordinariness." Creators Syndicate. 30 September 2008 <http://www.creators.com/opinion/froma-harrop/newman-embraced-ordinariness.html>.

[102] Source: "*Douglas Fairbanks*, by Jeffrey Vance: A review by Robert Gottlieb." *The New York Review of Books*. 23 February 2009 <http://www.nybooks.com/articles/22350>.

[103] Source: Anne E. Hill, *Cameron Diaz*, pp. 13, 20, 24-25.

[104] Source: Will Harris, "A Chat with Elliott Gould, Co-star of 'The Caller.'" Bullz-eye.com. 29 April 2009 <http://www.bullz-eye.com/movies/interviews/2009/elliott_gould.htm>.

[105] Source: Ed Halter, "A Jones for Indiana." *The Village Voice*. 3 July 2007 <http://www.villagevoice.com/nyclife/0727,halter,77128,15.html>.

[106] Source: Kieran Scott, *Leonardo diCaprio*, pp. 6, 24, 29, 32.

[107] Source: Robrt L. Pela, *Filthy: The Weird World of John Waters*, pp. 82-87. (Yes, "Robrt" is the correct spelling.)

[108] Source: David Carradine, *The Kill Bill Diary*, pp. 94, 100-101, 114.

[109] Source: Joe Franklin, *Up Late with Joe Franklin*, pp. 110-111.

[110] Source: Walter Oleksy, *Christopher Reeve*, pp. 33-34.

[111] Source: Yousuf Karsh, *Karsh: A Biography in Images*, p. 125.

[112] Source: Joe Garner, *Now Showing: Unforgettable Moments from the Movies*, p. 22.

[113] Source: David Hiltbrand, "Hugh Jackman brings epic sexiness to film epic 'Australia.'" *The Philadelphia Inquirer*. 26 November 2008 <http://www.popmatters.com/pm/article/66208-hugh-jackman-brings-epic-sexiness-to-film-epic-australia/>.

[114] Source: Rick Press: "Years after 'Lebowski,' The Dude abides." McClatchy Newspapers. 3 January 2008 <http://www.popmatters.com/pm/news/article/52661/years-after-lebowski-the-dude-abides/>.

[115] Source: Alec Baldwin, "Remembering My Father." 20 June 2009 <http://www.huffingtonpost.com/alec-baldwin/remembering-my-father_b_218441.html>.

[116] Source: Colin Covert, "Making the new 'Hulk' was an Abomination for Tim Roth." *Star Tribune* (Minneapolis, MN). 12 June 2008 <http://www.popmatters.com/pm/news/article/59687/making-the-new-hulk-was-an-abomination-for-tim-roth/>.

[117] Source: Tom Powers, *Steven Spielberg: Master Storyteller*, pp. 14, 46.

[118] Source: Anne E. Hill, *Sandra Bullock*, p. 35.

[119] Source: Groucho Marx, *Groucho Marx and Other Short Stories and Tall Tales*, p. 25.

[120] Source: Tanya Dean, *Theodor Geisel (Dr. Seuss)*, pp. 65-66.

[121] Source: Susan Netter, *Paul Newman and Joanne Woodward: An Unauthorized Biography*, p. 160.

[122] Source: Chaim Topol, compiler, *Topol's Treasury of Jewish Humor, Wit and Wisdom*, p. 47.

[123] Source: Leonard Maltin, *The Great Movie Comedians*, p. 186.

[124] Source: Walter Oleksy, *Christopher Reeve*, p. 48.

[125] Source: Susan Goldman Rubin, *Steven Spielberg: Crazy for Movies*, p. 48.

[126] Source: Chris Lemmon, *A Twist of Lemmon: A Tribute to My Father*, pp. 116-117.

[127] Source: Karman Kregloe, "Interview With Liz Feldman." 6 April 2008 <http://www.afterellen.com/people/2008/4/lizfeldman>.

[128] Source: Sharon Hadrian, "Pratibha Parmar Makes Change." 6 June 2007 <http://www.afterellen.com/people/2007/6/pratibhaparmar>.

[129] Source: Michael Jensen, "Interview with George Takei and Brad Altman." Afterelton.com. 18 June 2008 <http://www.afterelton.com/people/2008/6/georgetakei_bradaltman>.

[130] Source: Tom Danehy, "My friend is gone, three decades too early." *Tucson Weekly*. 8 November 2007 http://www.tucsonweekly.com/gbase/Opinion/Content?oid=oid:102916.

[131]Source: Bruce Vilanch, *Bruce! Adventures in the Skin Trade and Other Essays*, p. 67.

[132]Source: Paul Constant, "In a 'Star Trek' Outfit (How Not to Get Married)." *The Stranger*. 24 June 2008 <http://www.thestranger.com/seattle/Content?oid=606110 >. Also: Sally Kline, editor, *George Lucas: Interviews*, p. 51.

[133] Source: Marjorie Quinn, "Interview with Thomas Jane." The Celebrity Café. 2 October 2009 <http://thecelebritycafe.com/interviews/thomas_jane_2009.html>.

[134] Source: A. Ryan Nerz, *Jennifer Love Hewitt*, pp. 5, 29.

[135] Source: Sean Hepburn Ferrer, *Audrey Hepburn: An Elegant Spirit*, pp. 58, 68.

[136] Source: Yousuf Karsh, *Karsh: A Biography in Images*, p. 124.

[137] Source: Barbara Isenberg, *State of the Arts: California Artists Talk About Their Work*, p. 113.

[138]Source: Bruce Vilanch, *Bruce! Adventures in the Skin Trade and Other Essays*, pp. 33-34.

[139] Source: Susan Goldman Rubin, *Steven Spielberg: Crazy for Movies*, p. 52.

[140] Source: Luaine Lee, "Bob Balaban, behind the camera for HBO's 'Bernard and Doris.'" McClatchy-Tribune News Service. 12 February 2008 <http://www.popmatters.com/pm/news/article/54762/bob-balaban-behind-the-camera-for-hbos-bernard-and-doris/>.

[141] Source: Emma Brockes, "I gambled on my talent." *The Guardian*. 1 October 2008 <http://www.guardian.co.uk/music/2008/oct/01/classicalmusicandopera.usa.>

[142]Source: Walter Slezak, *What Time's the Next Swan?*, p. 113.

[143] Source: Art Linkletter, *Women are My Favorite People*, pp. 86-87.

[144] Source: Eli Wallach, *The Good, the Bad, and Me: In My Anecdotage*, p. 176.

[145] Source: Peter Guttmacher, *Legendary Horror Films*, p. 97.

[146]Source: John Gruen, *People Who Dance*, p. 129.

[147] Source: Karen Brandon, *Arnold Schwarzenegger*, pp. 46, 48, 85-86.

[148] Source: Veda Boyd Jones, *Ewan McGregor*, pp. 10, 25, 31, 47-48.

[149] Source: David Hiltbrand, "Meet the Dane who plays an immortal New York cop." 18 March 2008 <http://www.popmatters.com/pm/news/article/56265/meet-the-dane-who-plays-an-immortal-new-york-cop/>. This article originally appeared in *The Philadelphia Inquirer*.

[150] Source: Lonnie Hull DuPont, *Mike Myers*, pp. 13-14, 59.

[151]Source: Ben Hecht, *Charlie: The Improbable Life and Times of Charles MacArthur*, pp. 190-191.

[152]Source: Meredith Willson, *And There I Stood With My Piccolo*, p. 175.

[153] Source: Sean Hepburn Ferrer, *Audrey Hepburn: An Elegant Spirit*, p. 215.

[154]Source: John Waters, *Crackpot: The Obsessions of John Waters*, pp. 76-77.

[155] Source: Libby Brooks, "The day I met Patrick Swayze." *The Guardian*. 15 September 2009 <http://www.guardian.co.uk/film/2009/sep/15/patrick-swayze-dirty-dancing>.

[156]Source: Nancy Caldwell Sorel and Edward Sorel, *First Encounters*, p. 29.

[157]Source: Joey Adams, *The God Bit*, p. 67.

[158] Source: Stacey Stauffer, *Leonardo DiCaprio*, pp. 12, 17.

[159] Source: Stephen Cox, *The Munchkins Remember*, p. 18.

[160] Source: Ben Hecht, *Charlie: The Improbable Life and Times of Charles MacArthur*, p. 138.

[161] Source: David Brown, *Star Billing: Tell-Tale Trivia from Hollywood*, p. 60.

[162]Source: Miriam Weiss Meyer, project editor, *Top Picks: People*, p. 67.

[163] Source: Phil Hoad, 'I wanted freedom." *The Guardian*. 11 June 2008 <http://arts.guardian.co.uk/theatre/drama/story/0,,2284780,00.html>.

[164] Source: Maxine Marx, *Growing Up with Chico*, p. 97.

[165] Source: Kenn Duncan, *Divas: The Fabulous Photography of Kenn Duncan*, p. 50.

[166] Source: Nick Johnstone, *Johnny Depp: The Illustrated Biography*, p. 79.

[167]Source: Joe Bob Briggs, *Profoundly Disturbing: Shocking Movies That Changed History!*, p. 193.

[168]Source: Svetlana McLee Grody and Dorothy Daniels Lister, *Conversations With Choreographers*, p. 185.

[169] Source: Will Lawrence, "Abigail Breslin brings sunshine to *Definitely, Maybe.*" *The Times*. 31 January 2008 <http://entertainment.timesonline.co.uk/tol/arts_and_entertainment/film/article3278596.ece>.

[170] Source: Bill Zehme, *The Way You Wear Your Hat: Frank Sinatra and the Lost Art of Livin'*, pp. 43, 46.

[171]Source: Groucho Marx, *Groucho and Me*, pp. 330-331.

[172] Source: Colin Covert, "Q&A with 'No Country for Old Men' makers Joel and Ethan Coen." 9 November 2007 <http://www.popmatters.com/pm/news/article/50750/qa-with-no-country-for-old-men-makers-joel-and-ethan-coen/>. This article originally appeared in the *Star Tribune* (Minneapolis, MN).

[173] Source: Duane Damon, *Headin' for Better Times*, p. 13.

[174] Source: John G. Ives, *John Waters*, p. 55.

[175]Source: Andrew Hecht, *Hollywood Merry-Go-Round*, p. 40.

[176]Source: Andrew Hecht, *Hollywood Merry-Go-Round*, p. 118.

[177] Source: Jim McAvoy, *Tom Hanks*, pp. 18-19.

[178] Source: David Brown, *Star Billing: Tell-Tale Trivia from Hollywood*, p. 15.

[179] Source: Edward Edelson, *Great Kids of the Movies*, p. 2.

[180] Source: Steven Otfinoski, *Stan Lee: Comic Book Genius*, p. 92.

[181]Source: Bruce Campbell, *If Chins Could Kill: Confessions of a B Movie Actor*, pp. 96-97.

[182]Source: Penelope Gilliatt, *Jacques Tati*, p. 10.

[183]Source: Bob Bernotas, *Spike Lee: Filmmaker*, p. 33.

[184] Source: James Robert Parish, *Denzel Washington: Actor*, p. 10.

[185] Source: Matt Mueller, "What would his mother say?" *The Guardian*. 14 March 2008 <http://film.guardian.co.uk/interview/interviewpages/0,,2264916,00.html>.

[186] Source: Stuart Hample, "How I turned Woody Allen into a comic strip." *The Guardian*. 19 October 2009 <http://www.guardian.co.uk/film/2009/oct/18/woody-allen-comic-strip>.

[187] Source: Jon Chattman, "Paul Newman: Favorite Story to Tell." Huffington Post. 22 December 2008 <http://www.huffingtonpost.com/jon-chattman/favorite-story-to-tell_b_152501.html>.

[188] Source: John Miller, editor, *Legends: Women Who Have Changed the World*, pp. 46-47.

[189] Source: Carole Cadwalladr, "On the money." *The Observer*. 30 March 2008 <http://film.guardian.co.uk/interview/interviewpages/0,,2269263,00.html>.

[190] Source: Anne E. Hill, *Cameron Diaz*, p. 21.

[191] Source: Paul Parla and Charles P. Mitchell, *Screen Sirens Scream!*, p. 179.

[192] Source: H. Allen Smith, *Buskin' With H. Allen Smith*, p. 104.

[193] Source: Oscar Levant, *A Smattering of Ignorance*, pp. 127-128.

[194] Source: A. Ryan Nerz, *Jennifer Love Hewitt*, pp. 5-6, 17-18.

[195] Source: Harrison Pierce, "Welcome to the Dollhouse." *The Advocate*. 6 March 2009 <http://www.advocate.com/exclusive_detail_ektid74432.asp>.

[196] Source: Barbara Isenberg, *State of the Arts: California Artists Talk About Their Work*, pp. 14-15.

[197] Source: Bob Bernotas, *Spike Lee: Filmmaker*, p. 31.

[198] Source: Bill Zehme, *The Way You Wear Your Hat: Frank Sinatra and the Lost Art of Livin'*, pp. 55, 61, 63.

[199] Source: Richard Young, *Shooting Stars*, pp. 28-33.

[200] Source: Rick Bentley:, "No Joke: Lynn Collins' role was vital to 'Wolverine' story." McClatchy Newspapers. 4 May 2009 <http://www.popmatters.com/pm/article/92542-no-joke-lynn-collins-role-was-vital-to-wolverine-story/>.

[201] Source: Stefan Kanfer, "In Living Black-and-White." *City Journal*. Summer 2008. Vol. 18, No. 3. <http://www.city-journal.org/2008/18_3_urb-black_and_white_movies.html>.

[202] Source: Susan Netter, *Paul Newman and Joanne Woodward: An Unauthorized Biography*, pp. 146-147.

[203] Source: Bill Zehme, "Cameron Diaz Loves You." *Esquire*. 1 March 2002 <http://www.esquire.com/women/ESQ0402-APR_DIAZ>.

[204] Source: Joe Garner, *Made You Laugh*, p. 158.

[205] Source: Hank Gallo, *Comedy Explosion: A New Generation*, p. 21.

[206] Source: John Engstead, *Star Shots: Fifty Years of Pictures and Stories by One of Hollywood's Greatest Photographers*, pp. 40, 42.

[207] Source: Will Lawrence, "Renee Zellweger on George Clooney, 'Leatherheads' and independence." *The Times*. 3 April 2008 <http://entertainment.timesonline.co.uk/tol/arts_and_entertainment/film/article3668037.ece>.

[208] Source: Betty A. Marton, *Reubén Blades*, pp. 72-73.

[209] Source: Ben Primack, adapter and editor, *The Ben Hecht Show*, pp. 126-127.

[210] Source: Aaron Mesh, "David Gordon Green Loves a Good Mistake." *Willamette Week*. 26 March 2008 < http://wweek.com/editorial/3420/10731/>.

[211] Source: Nick Johnstone, *Johnny Depp: The Illustrated Biography*, pp. 39, 44, 55.

[212] Source: John Engstead, *Star Shots: Fifty Years of Pictures and Stories by One of Hollywood's Greatest Photographers*, p. 30.

[213]Source: Groucho Marx, *Groucho and Me*, pp. 228ff.

[214]Source: Nancy Caldwell Sorel and Edward Sorel, *First Encounters*, p. 35.

[215] Source: Keith Maher, "Diet hard! Ageing action heroes turn back the clock." *The Times*. 9 June 2007 <http://entertainment.timesonline.co.uk/tol/arts_and_entertainment/film/article1888554.ece>.

[216] Source: Joe Garner, *Made You Laugh*, p. 154.

[217]Source: Roger Ebert, "Ismail Merchant: In Memory." 26 May 2005 <http://rogerebert.suntimes.com/apps/pbcs.dll/article?AID=/20050526/PEOPLE/50526001>.

[218]Source: Paul Parla and Charles P. Mitchell, *Screen Sirens Scream!*, pp. 199-200.

[219]Source: Bruce Nash and Allan Zullo, *The Hollywood Walk of Shame*, p. 47.

[220] Source: Moira Macdonald, "'(500) Days' director creates a romantic comedy with chemistry you can dance to." *The Seattle Times*. 24 July 2009 <http://www.popmatters.com/pm/article/108808-500-days-director-creates-a-romantic-comedy-with-chemistry-you-can-d/>.

[221] Source: Dawn C. Chmielewski, "He knows all about being cool." Latimes.com. 18 October 2009 <http://www.latimes.com/business/la-fi-himi18-2009oct18,0,6526968.story>.

[222] Source: Jan Moir, "Joan Collins: low cunning and high drama." *The Telegraph*. 20 September 2007 <http://www.telegraph.co.uk/arts/main.jhtml?view=DETAILS&grid=&xml=/arts/2007/09/20/boloi116.xml>.

[223] Source: Catherine Shoard, "The tormented torso." *The Guardian*. 4 September 2008 <http://www.guardian.co.uk/film/2008/sep/04/actionandadventure>.

[224] Source: Andrew Osmond, "When animators get horny." *The Guardian*. 19 September 2008 <http://www.guardian.co.uk/film/2008/sep/19/animation>.

[225] Source: Peter Bogdanovich, *Peter Bogdanovich's Movie of the Week*, p. 75.

[226] Source: Meg Greene, *Will Smith*, pp. 18, 57.

[227] Source: Dick Richards, compiler, *The Wit of Peter Ustinov*, pp. 60-61.

[228] Source: John Miller, editor, *Legends: Women Who Have Changed the World*, pp. 98-99.

[229] Source: Richard Schickel, *Cary Grant: A Celebration*, pp. 9, 11.

[230] Source: Patty Fox, *Star Style: Hollywood Legends as Fashion Icons*, p. 17.

[231] Source: May Wale Brown, *Reel Life on Hollywood Movie Sets*, p. 6.

[232] Source: Frank Manchel, *The Box Office Clowns*, p. 65.

[233] Source: John G. Ives, *John Waters*, pp. 64-66.

[234] Source: H. Allen Smith, *Buskin' With H. Allen Smith*, p. 119.

[235] Source: Frank Manchel, *Yesterday's Clowns*, p. 23.

[236] Source: Ian Caddell, "For versatile Alan Arkin, a fine time to Get Smart." *The Georgia Straight*. 12 June 2008 <http://www.straight.com/article-149279/for-versatile-arkin-a-fine-time-get-smart>.

[237] Source: Richard Young, *Shooting Stars*, pp. 16-19.

[238] Source: Gay Bryant and Bockris-Wylie, *How I Learned to Like Myself*, p. 105.

[239] Source: Malinda Lo, "Interview With Donna Deitch." 3 June 2007 <http://www.afterellen.com/people/2007/6/donnadeitch>.

[240] Source: Peter Guttmacher, *Legendary Horror Films*, pp. 17, 19.

[241] Source: Frank Manchel, *Yesterday's Clowns*, pp. 26-27.

[242] Source: Bruce Campbell, *If Chins Could Kill: Confessions of a B Movie Actor*, p. 180.

[243] Source: Penelope Gilliatt, *Jacques Tati*, p. 83.

[244] Source: Frank Manchel, *The Box Office Clowns*, pp. 14-15.

[245] Source: Terry-Thomas, *Terry-Thomas Tells Tales*, p. 40.

[246] Source: Richard Schickel, *Cary Grant: A Celebration*, p. 52.

[247] Source: Leonard Maltin, *The Great Movie Comedians*, p. 42.

[248] Source: Rosanna Greenstreet, "Q&A: John Waters." *The Guardian*. 13 September 2008 <http://www.guardian.co.uk/lifeandstyle/2008/sep/13/4>.

[249] Source: Leslie Halliwell, *The Filmgoer's Book of Quotes*, p. 218.

[250] Source: Edward Edelson, *Funny Men of the Movies*, pp. 18-19.